TEN SESSIONS FOR A
CHILDREN'S CLUB

Scripture Union, 207–209 Queensway, Bletchley, Milton Keynes, MK2 2EB, United Kingdom.
Email: info@scriptureunion.org.uk
Website: www.scriptureunion.org.uk
Scripture Union Australia
Locked Bag 2, Central Coast Business Centre, NSW 2252, Australia
Website: www.scriptureunion.org.au
Scripture Union USA
PO Box 987, Valley Forge, PA 19482
Website: www.scriptureunion.org

Scripture quotations are from the Contemporary English Version © American Bible Society 1991, 1992, 1995. Anglicisations © British and Foreign Bible Society 1997, or from the Good News Bible © American Bible Society 1992, both published in the UK by HarperCollins*Publishers*. Used by permission. Or New International Version © International Bible Society, Anglicisations © 2001, used by permission of Hodder and Stoughton Limited.

British Library Cataloguing-in-Publication Data.
A catalogue record of this book is available from the British Library.

Printed and bound by Henry Ling
Cover Illustration by Toni Goffe
Internal illustrations by Pauline Adams
Cover and internal template design by Kevin Wade of kwgraphicdesign.
Internal layout by Richard Jefferson

Groups who took part in the trial:
Arrows, Yealhampton, Devon; **Bus Stop**, North Cheam Community Church, Surrey; **Comets**, North Cheam Baptist Church, Surrey; **Destiny Lunch Club**, St Chad C of E Infant and Nursery School, Derby; **Discovery Squad Lunch Club**, Beaufort Primary School, Derby; **Explorers**, Greasby Methodist Church, The Wirral; **JAM**, Thirlmere Church, St Albans; **Rock Solid Fun Club**, St Columba's Church, Darlington.

Scripture Union is an international Christian charity working with churches in more than 130 countries, providing resources to bring the good news of Jesus Christ to children, young people and families and to encourage them to develop spiritually through the Bible and prayer.

As well as our network of volunteers, staff and associates who run holidays, church-based events and school Christian groups, we produce a wide range of publications and support those who use our resources through training programmes.

Rocky Road is an eye level club programme, part of *eye level*, Scripture Union's project to catch up with children and young people who have yet to catch sight of Jesus.

For details of other eye level club resources and additional **Rocky Road** material visit www.scriptureunion.org.uk/eyelevel.

Contents

Join us on the Rocky Road

Sessions

This book is dedicated to the children, young people and leaders of the churches and groups where I have been privileged to serve God: Dorford Baptist Church, Dorchester; Dorchester Crusaders; Thirlmere Church, St Albans; St Albans Crusaders; The Family Trust, Maidstone; Boxley Road Evangelical Church, Maidstone; Sutton Schools Christian Workers Trust, Surrey; North Cheam Baptist Church, Surrey.

Join us on the Rocky Road

Aims of Rocky Road

Children need to know that Jesus loves them so much that he died for them. What's more, he longs for them to be his friend. Such a relationship makes all the difference to how a child understands life, develops as a person and as a member of their community. This is the BEST good news that we can ever share.

However, the majority of children know nothing about Jesus and have had little to do with his followers. But God has commissioned his followers to welcome children and to share his love with them and tell them his story. That's what **Rocky Road**, as another in the eye level programme, is all about.

The aims are:

- To welcome children into a regular club situation so that they can experience God's love in a community of Jesus' followers.
- To share the stories of the Bible, especially that of Moses, in a variety of ways.
- To challenge children to make a further step of commitment to Jesus.
- To build relationships with the family members of children in the club.
- To follow up the *Pyramid Rock* holiday club which explored the life of Joseph – although **Rocky Road** could be used independently. The material could be used for the first ten sessions of a new children's club or could provide a term's programme teaching for a well-established group.

	Session aims
Session 1 Slaves in Egypt	**Bible story**: The Egyptian king makes the Israelites his slaves (Exodus 1:6–22; 2:23b–25) **Aim**: To understand that, whatever happens to us, God knows about it and cares for us.
Session 2 The birth of Moses	**Bible story**: The birth of Moses (Exodus 2:1–10) **Aim**: To show how God had a plan to help the Israelites and that he has a plan for our lives too.
Session 3 God speaks to Moses	**Bible story**: God speaks to Moses at the burning bush (Exodus 3:1–15; 4:1–17,27–31) **Aim**: To help the children appreciate both the talking and listening aspects of their relationship with God.
Session 4 Let my people go!	**Bible story**: God sent plagues on the land of Egypt (Exodus 5–11) **Aim**: To help the group see that God is more powerful than anyone or anything. We can trust in God's power to help us when things are hard.
Session 5 The Passover	**Bible story**: The Passover (Exodus 12:1–42) **Aim**: To hear how the Israelites were saved by the Passover lamb and relate this to the saving death of Jesus.
Session 6 Crossing the Red Sea	**Bible story**: The Israelites cross the Red Sea (Exodus 13:17–22; 14:5–31; 15:19–21) **Aim**: To understand that God was with the Israelites to lead and guide them and that he will be with us too.
Session 7 God provides manna and quail	**Bible story**: God provides the Israelites with manna and quail (Exodus 16) **Aim**: To realise that everything we have is given to us by God and we should thank him for it.
Session 8 God gives laws to his people	**Bible story**: The Ten Commandments are given to Moses (Exodus 19; 20:1–17) **Aim**: To show that God knows the best way for people to live and so we should keep his laws.
Session 9 The golden calf	**Bible story**: Aaron builds a golden calf and the people worship it (Exodus 32) **Aim**: To recognise how easy it is to put other things before God. God is living and active; we should put him first and worship him.
Session 10 Spies explore Canaan	**Bible story**: Moses sends twelve spies to explore the land of Canaan (Numbers 13; 14:1–24, Joshua 1:1–9) **Aim**: To realise that trusting and following God is a lifelong commitment.

How to use this teaching

⊛ Part 1: Gather together

(5–30 minutes)
Gather together is a selection of fun activities involving movement, games, craft and action whilst introducing the session's aim and story. This is a good way for everyone to enjoy being together whilst letting off steam at the beginning of the session. Vary your choice of activities according to the mood of the children as they arrive, the type of venue you have, the number of helpers and the time available.

At least one of the games each week is suitable for a small group while others would work well with younger children or involve pencil and paper. Often the first game is one which children can join in at any time (for example a round-the-walls quiz), and this is useful if the children tend to arrive in dribs and drabs. On occasions you could start with the craft activity which gives an opportunity to chat to the children and catch up with their news as well as allowing for latecomers.

For ease of reference all the games and the main craft are in this section – but this doesn't mean they have to go first! For example, you may prefer to start with a quick game and then give the majority of your time to the main teaching, finishing with more games and craft. It's often good to swap things around and include different activities (such as a verse to *Learn and remember*) just to give that edge of excitement and anticipation.

> An activity for a small group is marked ⊕.
> An activity for younger children is marked .

⊛ Part 2: Setting off

(5 minutes)
In each session *Setting off* shows how to link different items of walking equipment with the Israelites' journey to the Promised Land. *Setting off* can be a fun way to calm the children down after the excitement of games and also recap what has happened so far along the **Rocky Road**.

⊛ Part 3: Explore the Bible

(10-20 minutes)
Explore the Bible is where the children hear the next episode of Moses' story. This section has two different storytelling ideas as well as a quiz to reinforce the salient points. (For hints and tips on storytelling see pages 8–9.) The stories for sessions 2–6 are also covered by the popular *Prince of Egypt* video – but do watch the relevant excerpt before you show it to check that it is suitable for your group and covers all you want it to say. If your group enjoys quizzes, make the desert scoring system (see pages 56–58, 63), which can be used throughout the series.

⊛ Part 4: Make a discovery

(10–20 minutes)
Make a discovery is the main teaching session based on the Bible story. To include some sort of biblical application should be the priority of your work with the children or they will simply end up knowing the story of Moses without realising that there are lessons they can apply to their lives.

Included in *Make a discovery* are some Bible verses for the children to *Learn and remember*. Most of these *Learn and remember* verses are taught in one session and then used and recapped in the following one. Feel free to teach the verse earlier or later in your session – wherever you feel is most appropriate for your group. If you don't have time to include them all, then just pick one or two from the series and concentrate on those.

Three of the *Learn and remember verses* (sessions 1,8 and 10) are available in song form, downloadable from www.scriptureunion.org.uk/music. These songs have been written in a contemporary style which the children will recognise and enjoy.

⊛ Part 5: Travel further

(The length of time will vary for each activity)
This section includes ideas to help the children respond through creative prayer. Some of these ideas include things to make and so you could substitute them for your usual craft slot. Even if you find you are often short of time near the end of your club, do include a prayer idea, at least sometimes.

Sometimes there was almost too much in the sessions!

Sarah, Greasby

Songs

Have you ever tried singing in your children's club? There are lots of excellent tracks on children's praise and worship CDs which you can sing along with even if you don't have a musician. Songs can be included to start your session off, as part of *Make a discovery* or at the end. Look out for songs which involve actions but be sure to include some quieter, reflective songs as well as more lively ones. Here are a few suggestions about God's power, faith, obedience and guidance, which are the main themes of **Rocky Road**. Be careful though to ensure that you are not putting words in the children's mouths which they cannot personally mean.

'Call to me' (*LFE*)
'For God so loved the world' (*KS* 464)
'Great big God' (*Vineyard*)
'I need faith' (*KS* 168)
'How did Moses cross the Red Sea?' (*KS* 112, *JP* 83)
'You call me to be yours (I can't see your face)' (*Vineyard*)
'I'm gonna jump up and down' (*SH* 03)
'King of all' (*RU*)
'Now and forever' (*LFE*)
'Safe in the Father's hands' (*KS* 290)
'Taller than the mountains' (*RU*)
'Twelve men went to spy' (*JP* 261)
'Twisting back in time' (*LFE*)
'When you make a mistake' (*RU*)
'You need to natter to God' (*KS* 798)

JP (*Junior Praise*)
KS (*Kidsource*)
LFE (SU *Light for Everyone* CD)
RU (SU *Reach Up!* CD)
SH (*Spring Harvest*)

NEW!
Bible Codecrackers: Moses
£3.99 64pp
The story of Moses using Bible text, retold story and challenging puzzles makes him live for 8-11s in a fun way.

Moses the Brave Leader
£1.99 32pp
A puzzle book for 5-7s which tells the story of Moses in a fun way.

10 RULZ Andy Bianchi
£4.99 128pp
The Ten Commandments as you've never seen them before! Cartoons, story and links with real life today makes this a can't-put-down book for 8-11s.

Use these books as a final gift to each child who has been in the club or use throughout the series.

(Prices correct at the time of going to print.)

All of these are available from good local Christian bookshops or from SU Mail Order: Scripture Union Mail Order, PO Box 5148, Milton Keynes MLO, MK2 2YX
Tel: 0845 07 06 006 Fax: 01908 856020
Web: www.scriptureunion.org.uk

Storytelling

Telling the story of how God rescued and led Moses and the Israelites is an essential feature of the journey along the **Rocky Road**. Every week another episode is added as the people travel from slavery in Egypt to the border of the Promised Land. However, many people feel that they are not gifted in storytelling and prefer to watch a video or read the story from a children's book of Bible stories. The aim of this page is to help you rekindle what might be a dying art form.

✿ Know the facts

Often we think that we know a Bible story – after all, we heard it when we were children! But were you aware of how God came down on Mount Sinai? What about the different excuses Moses made at the burning bush and the signs he performed? And what did the 12 spies go and spy? Don't simply rely on your memory – read the biblical text through before you look in a children's Bible.

As you read, you might find it helpful to jot down the order of events, key facts, key people and content of speeches. In **Rocky Road** there are some long Bible passages (for example, the ten plagues) so you will need to consider whether all the intricate detail is necessary or if it will detract from the main storyline. If the story contains difficult words or unfamiliar concepts think about how these can be simplified or explained as part of the story. For example, say 'Moses went to see Pharaoh – the king of Egypt' or 'God told the people not to collect any manna on the Sabbath because it was their special holy day like our Sunday'.

✿ Different story methods

Most children learn through seeing and doing rather than by hearing alone. Involving different learning styles as you tell a story can greatly help a child's concentration and retention of the facts. If you can draw well or have access to picture books you could display illustrations (use the SU publication *How to Cheat at Visual Aids* which contains pictures of Bible characters and scenes).

If the story has some repeated key words ask the children to listen out for them and then respond with actions, or play a team game and every time a particular word is mentioned the children race round their team and back to their place. Story bags are increasingly popular in school and you could make one of these yourself and include different items that feature in the story. If there are a lot of nouns, then think about playing a drawing game before you tell the story or play 'hangman' as you go through. Another fun way is to read the story straight from the Bible and then reread it again with some mistakes for the children to spot. Children love acting and miming – particularly if everyone can be involved in a crowd scene. Alternatively ask leaders to act or be interviewed as if they had been with Moses. If you are more creative then make some simple puppets by dressing wooden spoons or sticking faces to traffic cones.

You will probably find that different leaders enjoy different methods so vary what you do through the series to give the children different learning experiences.

✿ Start and finish well

Even if you have wonderful pictures or exciting props and puppets you will still have to relate the story in your own words. If your group has been involved in energetic games or the children are still sticky from craft then keeping their attention is important. Start with confidence, having planned your first sentence in advance so that it grabs their imagination and finds them eager to discover what happens.

The final sentence is important too – you don't want the story to simply fade away. Perhaps this sentence could sum up your main teaching point (for example, '… and so the people heard all of God's commandments' or '… Joshua knew that he would lead them into the Promised Land'.).

✿ Telling the story

As you tell the story use your face and voice to convey different feelings such as being happy, sad, proud, angry, surprised or worried. Try to change your pitch and tone for different characters or situations they find themselves in. If someone is running or excited then speak more quickly, or if they are pondering something then speak more slowly. As you reach the climax of the story or just before something exciting happens pause and then speak in a quieter voice. Move around your stage area as the story changes venue and use your body and hands to mime actions such as jumping away from the frogs, packing to leave Egypt or picking up manna in the desert.

✸ Use your voice

Make sure you speak naturally and sound interested in the story yourself – if you have to read it then know the script well enough to add expression.

And finally – there is nothing that can take the place of practice, practice and even more practice!

✸ Storytelling ideas

Have a look at the different storytelling methods used in this material:

1   Story bag (sessions 1 and 5)
2   Using pictures (sessions 3 and 4)
3   Acting/Interview by leaders (sessions 3, 7 and 9)
4   Using puppets (sessions 2 and 9)
5   Children acting or miming (sessions 4, 6 and 10)
6   Spotting mistakes (session 2)
7   Responding to phrases with actions or words (sessions 1, 5, 7 and 10)
8   Guessing key words (session 6)
9   Using sound effects (session 8)
10 Rhythm and rhyme (session 8)

Getting to know you

⊛ Building relationships

The children you'll meet at **Rocky Road** live in a fast-moving, sophisticated, technology-orientated world, dominated by screens. There is so much 'stuff' demanding their attention. Rather than trying to compete with that sort of environment, offer them what they are often missing elsewhere – real communication. Concentrate on the unique opportunity you have to build relationships, listen to them, talk with them, and give them time as you show them God's love in action. That way they will get to know you, each other and God on their **Rocky Road** adventure, and have a great time too!

⊛ Top tips for sharing Jesus with children

• **Build strong friendships**. Be genuinely interested in their lives, homes, interests, what happens at school. These friendships will be bridges across which Jesus can walk! Ensure that these children know that you appreciate and respect them.

• **Be informed** about what is happening at school and home – it's useful to be in the know about sports days, class excursions or family events, and these may explain why the children are excited or tired, or both!

• **Get to know the children's families**: understand their home lives, and help their parents (or whoever is responsible for their care) know what they are learning. Children can never be divorced from their home backgrounds. Avoid talking about Mum and Dad. It's best to refer to Mum or Dad or even, 'whoever looks after you at home'.

• **Remember birthdays**, or ask someone else to take on the responsibility of noting dates and preparing cards, perhaps for the other children to sign.

• **Do as you say!** The children need to see you model what you teach them. Your friendship with Jesus matters. How else will the children see what it means in practice to be in a relationship with him?

• **Encourage everyone to join in** – adults and children alike. Create a 'we're in this together' feel to the sessions, rather than 'them and us' – avoid organising activities that adults stand and watch. Relax, have fun and learn with the children – *' ...aim to give children the best hour of their week!'* Dave Connelly, Frontline Church.

• **Mind your language!** Avoid jargon words (eg sin, grace or churchy words) and explain what you mean by things like prayer.

• **Use illustrations from everyday life** to explain concepts. Jesus taught complex truths in simple ways (for example you can't see wind, but you can see the effects that it has; it's the same with the Holy Spirit). You will need to think about this before the club begins.

• **Grow the children's confidence with the Bible** and explain how to read it. Why don't we often start at page 1? How do we use the contents page? (Younger children find this very hard.) What are the differences between chapters and verses, or the Old and New Testaments? How do you explain that the Bible is one big story – God's story – in different bits?

• **Talk about Jesus**, rather than God, where possible. The Gospels give us clear pictures of what he is like and these are far easier to grasp than the idea of God being 'up there' but invisible. Children have some very woolly ideas about God, but there is less room for manoeuvre when it comes to Jesus! **Rocky Road** is based on the Old Testament but Jesus is naturally introduced at several points throughout the programme.

• **Apply the Bible teaching appropriately**: For example, when thinking about how Moses showed God's power to Pharaoh, ask about times when children need God's power to help them – in a school lesson, when someone is unkind. This makes sense to them.

• **Allow children to make responses** that are appropriate for them, their understanding and their backgrounds. Don't rush straight in with, 'Do you want to follow Jesus?' That should be a decision that lasts for life, and they need to recognise what it entails. For many children, there are a number of commitments as their understanding grows.

• **Have fun together!** The children need to catch something of the 'life in all its fullness' that Jesus spoke about.

Working with small groups

⊛ Practicalities

• Children are all different. Respect their differences.
• Make sure any child with a special need is catered for.
• Make sure children know they can come to you with any questions.
• Make sure that children are comfortable. Cold, hard floors do not encourage positive discussion. Cushions, mats or comfortable chairs can make all the difference. Sometimes, everyone lying on their tummies in a star shape can create a fantastic atmosphere – their teacher at school is unlikely to do this.
• Keep good eye contact with every child.
• In the group, watch out for children who are on the edge.
• Don't talk down to children – talk with them. This means getting to their level, physically and verbally.
• Don't always rush to fill silences while children are thinking of responses.
• Validate all responses, either by a further question or ask others what they think, especially if you don't agree with the initial comment or answer.
• If lots of children want to talk, pass an object round – only the child holding the object can speak.
• Encourage children to listen to each other (something they might find quite difficult).
• Be prepared to admit that you don't know the answer to a question, but say that you'll find out the answer, if appropriate.

⊛ Asking questions

There are plenty of opportunities in **Rocky Road** for asking the children questions about the Bible passage and encouraging their thinking about God. A discussion is most appropriate when the children are in small groups as they don't need to wait as long for an opportunity to speak.

Ever thought about the kinds of questions you ask people? The same question can be asked in many different ways, and force the person being asked the question to give certain kinds of answers.

?? Rhetorical

If you ask, 'Isn't it great to have ice cream?', it is a **rhetorical question**, implying the expected answer. It brings out the right answer for the benefit of others.

?? Closed

If you ask, 'Do you like coming to **Rocky Road**?', it is a **closed question**, mainly allowing for 'Yes' or 'No'. It encourages contributions and assesses what the children think.

?? Factual

If you ask, 'What did God give the Israelites to eat in the desert?', it is a **factual question**, requiring basic information. It encourages contributions and establishes the facts.

?? Open

If you ask, 'Why did Pharaoh make the Israelites slaves?', it is an **open question**, allowing broad expression. It encourages discussion and indicates what the children think.

?? Experience

If you ask, 'Have you ever felt like you were in a hopeless situation – like when the Egyptians were chasing the Israelites whose path was blocked by the Red Sea?', it is an **experience question**, for sharing views or feelings. It encourages discussion and helps children to apply the teaching personally.

?? Leading

If you ask, 'What have you learnt at **Rocky Road**, Anna?', it is a **leading question** aimed at getting a specific answer from someone. It indicates learning and understanding and encourages contributions.

Think about when you might use these types of questions in your group. Go through each question with your team and decide when it is appropriate and when it is inappropriate to use certain kinds of questions.

Helping children respond

 Being Jesus' friend

Rocky Road introduces children to people from the Old Testament who were trying (and often failing!) to follow God. The children will find out about the awesome God who loves and cares for us, and who came as Jesus Christ to rescue us and help us to be his friends. They will see that we should always thank him, and obey him. They will also learn that Jesus can forgive us for the wrong we have done. This may prompt the children to want to know Jesus personally.

• They rarely need long explanations, just simple answers to questions.

• Talk to them in a place where you can be seen by others.

• Never put pressure on children to respond in a particular way, just help them take one step closer to Jesus when they are ready. We don't want them to respond just to please us!

• Remember, many children make a commitment to Christ, followed by further commitments as they mature and their understanding grows.

• Many children just need a bit of help to say what they want to say to God. Here is a suggested prayer they could use to make a commitment to Jesus:

> *Jesus, I want to be your friend.*
> *Thank you that you love me.*
> *Thank you for living in the world and dying on a cross for me.*
> *I'm sorry for all the wrong things I have done.*
> *Please forgive me and let me be your friend.*
> *Please let the Holy Spirit help me be like you.*

Reassure them that God hears us when we talk with him and has promised to forgive us and help us be his friends.

 What next?

Children need help to stick with Jesus, especially if their parents don't believe.

• Assure them that God wants them to talk with him, whatever they want to say. Give them some prayer ideas.

• Encourage them to keep coming to Christian activities, not necessarily on Sundays – their church might have to be the midweek club or a school lunch-time club.

• Reading the Bible will be easier with something like *Snapshots* – but you need to support them if they are to keep it up. It may be appropriate to give them a Bible as well. Make sure that this is not seen as a reward for becoming a Christian.

• Keep praying and maintain your relationship with them and their family wherever possible.

 Some booklets from Scripture Union that may help

Friends with Jesus
A booklet explaining what it means to make a commitment to follow Jesus for under-8s.
1 84427 141 2 (single) £0.99
1 84427 144 7 (pack of 20) £15.00

Me+Jesus
A booklet explaining what it means to make a commitment to follow Jesus for 8 to 10s.
1 84427 142 0 (single) £0.99
1 84427 145 5 (pack of 20) £15.00

Jesus=friendship forever
A booklet explaining what it means to make a commitment to follow Jesus for 10 to 12s.
1 84427 143 9 (single) £0.99
1 84427 146 3 (pack of 20) £15.00

What Jesus did
D Abrahall
A book exploring Jesus, ideal for those with special needs.
1 84427 005 X (single) £2.00
1 84427 006 8 (pack of 5 with teachers' guide) £8.00

Snapshots
Bible reading for 8- to 11-year-olds
£3.00 single copy
UK £11.00 annual subscription
£15.00 packs of 6
£0.99 4–week challenge (1 84427 086 6)

(Prices are correct at the time of going to press.)
For a simple commitment card, visit the eye level website: www.scriptureunion.org.uk/eyelevel

Sharing your faith

So many people put their trust in Jesus because they have heard how important he is to someone else. You have a great opportunity to share with the children what Jesus means to different people, and also to show by the way you live your own life that Jesus really is alive! Here are some pointers to bear in mind when you're talking with children about what Jesus means to you:

• Make sure you don't use Christian jargon or concepts that just don't make sense – 'Inviting Jesus into your heart' might suggest to some children that Jesus is only welcome in a bit of them. The idea of a person you can't see living inside your body can be a bit spooky!

• Remember you are talking to children whose experience of life is not as broad as an adult's, so their uncertainties and questions are different. Address their issues by referring to experiences which are relevant to them. This is not necessarily just what it was like for you when you were a child! But, for example, the emotions you experienced when you recently changed job may be very similar to those of a child changing school. God was with you then, so can be with a child.

• Speak about Jesus as someone you know and are enthusiastic about.

• Make reference to what the Bible says in a way that makes a child want to read the Bible for themselves – sound enthusiastic about what God has said to us. Hold the Bible with respect and read with interest. Tell a Bible story briefly to explain a point.

• Be brief and speak with simple sentences, using appropriate language.

• Be honest, talking about the good and the bad times. God doesn't always give answers straightaway or the answers we want.

• It is important to talk about what Jesus means to us now and not when we first came to know him dozens of years ago.

If you are involved in an up-front presentation, there are some other points to consider:

• An interview process is less intense and invites the children to engage with what the interviewee is saying.

• Include questions or information about subjects such as favourite colours, food, team, job, hopes, worst moments, as well as a favourite Bible character or story. Think what a child is curious about. 'Normal' information communicates that being a Christian is all about Jesus being with us all the time, being normal!

• Not everyone's experience will be appropriate, however dramatic it might be! Long and complicated stories will lose children. A wide age range of children will also determine what is suitable.

• Use someone's story which is relevant to the theme of the day.

• Over the weeks, choose a variety of people with different experiences to share what Jesus means to them.

• It would be worth the team hearing what is going to be said in advance, if someone's experience is going to raise questions that may be a challenge to answer.

Whether you're speaking in front of the whole club, or one child, you should be ready to tell your story. Think beforehand about what you are going to say, just as you would practise music or drama. It isn't a speech but there is no excuse for rambling.

Practical considerations

It is important to think about child protection when running your club. If your midweek club has already been in existence for some time, you have probably made all the necessary arrangements. However, if you are just starting up a midweek club, there is child protection advice on the Scripture Union website. For advice specific to running a holiday club, see the child protection section in *Pyramid Rock*.

What to do after Rocky Road

❀ Step one – time to think

Hopefully **Rocky Road** has made you think about how you run activities and reach out to children in your community. Before the end of the **Rocky Road** series, plan a review with anyone who helped. Be as honest as you can and dream dreams!
• What did the children enjoy about **Rocky Road**?
• What was different compared to your previous activities for children?
• Were there more small-group activities? How did they work?
• Was there more Bible input than before?
• What worked really well or didn't work?
• What did the leaders enjoy?
• What did you discover about each other's gifts for working with children? Was there an unknown storyteller or someone especially good at welcoming children?

Write down the most important answers. Talk about what you should do next.

❀ Step two – moving on

Don't be afraid to develop what you provide for children. If **Rocky Road** encouraged you to run a midweek or Saturday club for the first time and it worked, plan to carry on. You may need extra help, especially if some people can't commit themselves weekly. Perhaps you could continue your club next term or maybe a monthly Saturday/Sunday special, using another Scripture Union programme.

Discuss how you might contact new children. What are your links with the local school(s) or neighbourhood groups? Could you publicise your group through the local paper or library? How could the children who already come be encouraged to bring their friends? Just how many more children can you cope with?

❀ Step three – building on Rocky Road

One of the aims of **Rocky Road** is to bring children who don't usually have much contact with a Christian community into a Christian activity. If this worked for you, build on the final **Rocky Road** session and get to know the

children's families by running a parents' special event. Family games work well, either games to play as families or everyone all together. Any family activity that offers food will be popular! Alternatively, some churches have explored parenting groups. In one place a church football team has developed from fathers of children who started coming to a church children's club. Be imaginative and find out what other churches have done in your area. Maybe you could do something together.

Whatever you do, try to maintain contact with children, to sustain and grow your relationships. You may wish to visit them at home, to deliver a birthday card or to let parents know the starting date for next term or to invite families to a family event or special service such as a carol service. If you do so, make sure parents are happy for you to come and contact them to arrange a time for your visit.

❀ Other programmes

Streetwise, Awesome! and *Clues2Use*, eight-session programmes similar in aim and design to **Rocky Road**, are already available. *Streetwise*, with an accompanying DVD (based on the *Luke Street* video), introduces children to the inhabitants of various houses Jesus visited, using Luke's Gospel. *Awesome!* and its accompanying DVD (based on the *Signposts* video) find signs to who Jesus is in the Gospel of John. *Clues2Use* which follows on from the *Landlubbers* holiday club programme is based on Luke's Gospel and uses the *Jesus Quest* DVD.

Look out for *Wastewatchers*, a five-day environmental holiday club programme based on Genesis 1 and 2 and John's Gospel, as children discover God's transformation in creation and in the lives of all those who follow Christ.

All of these are available from good local Christian bookshops or from SU Mail Order: Scripture Union Mail Order, PO Box 5148, Milton Keynes MLO, MK2 2YX
Tel: 0845 07 06 006 Fax: 01908 856020
Web: www.scriptureunion.org.uk

Extra activities

The first and last few minutes of a club can be the most important! Your first conversation with a child helps to settle them, for them to be open to God. You represent Jesus: your welcome is his welcome. The end of the club may be what they remember best, so make the most of the time.

✱ A few guidelines

• Choose the right opening question for the right day: if it's the weekend, keep school conversation to a minimum.
• Be led by the child. Don't probe where they don't want to talk.
• Allow a conversation to develop rather than just asking questions.
• Help others join in as they join the group.
• Tell the children about your day to build friendships and make it less like a grilling.

✱ Questions about school

What was the best thing that happened? Did anything funny happen? What did you have for dinner? What's the food like at your school?

✱ General questions

What have you seen on television/read/done recently? What are you doing this weekend? How's your football team doing? Tell me about your family/pets/what you do in your spare time.

✱ Ideas to end the club

A routine pattern to the end may be useful.

✱ In groups

• Chat about what they will do at home/later/during the week.
• A quick recap of the Bible teaching to help them remember/apply it.
• Pray for the week ahead.

✱ Together

• Recap the Bible teaching and allow a moment to think about it again.
• Sing the same song each week which has become the theme song for the club.

One after-school club always concludes with a short prayer followed by a 'wind-up Amen' where everyone starts saying 'Amen' softly and ends up shouting it. One classroom teacher asked a leader of the club what it was that the children always shouted at the end! It was a good opening to share about prayer!

✱ Time-fillers

1 Turn everyone's name round and enjoy the different sounds! (Nhoj Htims, Enna Senoj).
2 I Spy. For very young children play 'I spy with my colour eye', with objects of a certain colour.
3 Who can… wiggle their ears, touch their nose with their tongue, recite the alphabet backwards, wiggle their eyebrows and so on.
4 Dice games: have ready-made cards with questions to be answered when the numbers are rolled. For example:
Favourites: 1 – food; 2 – pop group; 3 – team; 4 – TV programme; 5 – story; 6 – colour.
Home: 1 – family; 2 – rooms; 3 – pets; 4 – food; 5 – outside the house; 6 – favourite room.
Favourite food: 1 – sandwich; 2 – drink; 3 – breakfast; 4 – biscuits; 5 – snack; 6 – worst food.
5 Moses says (Simon says with a **Rocky Road** flavour)
6 'I went to the park (supermarket, football match) and I saw…' Each person recites the growing list and adds an item.
7 Mime things you do at home – others must guess, eg watching TV, turning on a tap, cleaning teeth.
8 Challenge the group to make a human sculpture of household objects, eg a chair, knife and fork, clock, bathroom.

If the children's arrival is staggered, you may want to have a general activity that they can join in as they arrive. Or you might want to have an ongoing activity, which the children can do as a group craft.

1

Session 1
SLAVES IN EGYPT

Bible story: The Israelites were made slaves in Egypt (Exodus 1:6–22; 2:23b–25)

Aim: To understand that, whatever happens to us, God knows about it and cares for us.

Notes for you: This story starts some 400 years before the birth of Moses when Joseph's family move to live in Egypt (Genesis chapters 46–50). As time passed the number of Israelites grew until they became a great nation. When Pharaoh realised how strong they were he was worried they might cause a civil war so he forced them to become slaves – working in his fields, making bricks, building houses, cities and maybe even the pyramids. However, rather than this controlling the Israelites their numbers grew and Pharaoh decided he had to take more drastic action. Firstly he ordered the midwives to kill all newborn boys and when this didn't work he ordered that any baby boys be thrown into the River Nile – in other words to be sacrificed to the river god.

Gather together

◖◗1  Egyptian anagrams

(10 minutes)

What you need
• Ten (or more) anagrams associated with Egypt, each written on a separate card
• Blu-tack
• Pens and paper

What you do
Stick your Egyptian anagrams up round the room. Give each child a pen and paper. The children work individually or in pairs to work out the anagrams and write down their answers. The person with the most correct answers is the winner. If you don't have time to play this game in your first session then keep it 'in reserve' as it will be appropriate until the Israelites have left Egypt (session 5). This game gets you all into the 'Egyptian' mood.

Possible anagrams are:
rested – desert; reivR liNe – River Nile; rapmidy – pyramid; dans – sand; malp rete – palm tree; lamec – camel; pinhxs – sphinx; roCia – Cairo; hhaarPo – Pharaoh; briacA – Arabic

📎 I hid the words in places that weren't obvious (ceilings, on the underside of tables, behind doors). The children really worked well together in teams to solve the puzzles. 📎
Dave, North Cheam

◖◗2 Tangle

(5–10 minutes)

What you do
Divide your group into teams of about eight children. Each team stands in a circle facing inwards. Everyone closes their eyes, puts their right hand into the circle and grabs hold of any other hand. They repeat this with their left hand and then open their eyes. The object of the game is for the group to untangle themselves into one or more circles without letting go of their hands. This introduces the idea of being enslaved in some way.

◖◗3 Jailer

(10 minutes)

What you do
Choose one player to be the 'jailer'. Explain that this is a simple tagging game. Any player who is tagged by the jailer has to stand along one wall with an arm outstretched, touching the wall. These prisoners are now 'chained' to the wall in a line. Untagged players can set them free by running under their outstretched arms. However, this is at the risk of being caught and tagged themselves. Play until everyone is chained to the wall and then let the jailer run under all the arms to release them. You will need one 'jailer' for every eight players. Like the previous game, this game suggests the captivity theme.

◖◗4  Make an...
...Egyptian headdress

(10–15 minutes)

You will need for each headdress
• Strip of card 60 x 3 cm

1

- Piece of blue crêpe paper, 50 x 50 cm cut as shown
- Strips of yellow or gold paper

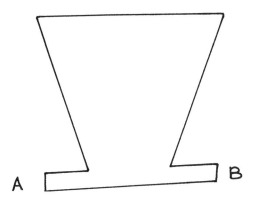

A   B

What you do
Glue the strip of card to the BACK of the headdress between points A and B. There will be some overlap at either end. Glue yellow or gold strips of paper to make vertical stripes on the headdress. Fit A to B around the child's head. Arrange the flap to cover the child's hair.

There are opportunities to use your headgear as a prop in future weeks in games and drama.

The idea for this came from *Here's one I made earlier*, Scripture Union.

⑥ *This was very simple to do – even for the younger age group.* ⑨
Elis, Yealhampton

For an alternative craft idea have a look at the prayer pyramids (pages 19 and 59).

Setting off

(2–5 minutes)
Ask the children for ideas of people who care for them. What sort of things are these people interested in? Do they want to know happy/good things as well as bad/sad things? Explain that things didn't always go well for God's people, the Israelites, but he was still interested and still cared for them. Use one of the suggestions below to tell the story from **Exodus 1:6–22 and 2:23b–25** and then recap using the quiz.

Explore the Bible

⊕1 Good news or bad news?

(10 minutes)

What you do
Read or tell the story from **Exodus 1:6–22 and 2:23b–25**. As you read, whenever something good happens ask the children to give a thumbs up and when something bad happens a thumbs down. Alternatively, ask the children to walk to opposite ends of your room for good or bad.

For example: Lots of Israelites = good; Pharaoh scared of a war = bad; Israelites become slaves = bad; families grew larger = good and so on.

At the end ask the children whether they think things were mainly good or mainly bad.

⊕2 ⊕Use a story bag

(10 minutes)

What you need
- A colourful bag containing about six objects related to the story (for example, camel, crown, family photograph, chain, brick, nurse's hat, baby doll)

What you do
Before the session, place the objects in your story bag. As you mention the different people, places and things in the story display the objects as a visual aid. Try to do this with a sense of anticipation by saying things like 'A new king came to power… I wonder if there's anything in here that a king might wear…' Afterwards put all the items back into your bag and invite the children to pull them out and tell you where they fitted in. The story is found in **Exodus 1:6–22 and 2:23b–25**.

⊕3 Quiz

(10 minutes)
Below are some suggested questions for a quiz. If you plan to use them as written you need to

A child's world: This is a violent story although the violence is not emphasised. Children used to seeing scenes on the TV screen of distressed parents, frightened children and human tragedy will, sadly, find it familiar. The fact that God is there, knows about such suffering and cares is a powerful truth to grasp, even though the imponderable question of why such suffering happens remains with us. If you have lots of new children, they may be reluctant to share anything deep that troubles them. Their trust in you should develop through this programme.

1

make sure you cover all the points in your storytelling! Make the quiz system on pages 56–58, 63 and then use it each week.

What you need
- 10 copies of the outer card (from page 56) numbered 1–10
- 2 copies of each of the points cards (from pages 57–58, 63)
- A board to mount the quiz on
- Blu-tack

What you do
Before the session use Blu-tack to attach the points cards (in a random order) to your board – perhaps in a 1–2–3–4 formation so they look like a pyramid. Cover each points card with an outer card, numbered 1–10.

Divide the group into two teams and ask the questions below to each team alternately. When a child gets the answer right they choose a number and you remove the outer card to reveal how many points they have scored for their team. When all the questions have been asked add up the points to see which team has won. It might be easier to ask one child from each team to keep hold of their points cards so that adding up is easier.

1 Which country were the Israelites living in? *Egypt*
2 Why was the king of Egypt afraid? *There might be a war with the Israelites*
3 What did the king decide to do? *Make the Israelites his slaves*
4 What sort of work did he make them do? *Building, making bricks, working in fields*
5 When the king realised that there were still too many Israelites, who did he call for? *The midwives/nurses*
6 What did the king want the midwives/nurses to do? *Kill all newborn baby boys*
7 Did the midwives obey the king? *No*
8 How did God reward the midwives/nurses? *Gave them children of their own*
9 When the population continued to grow, what was the king's new evil plan? *To drown the baby boys*
10 Who knew everything that was happening and cared for the Israelites? *God*

Make a discovery
(10 minutes)

What you need
- A heavy rucksack (for example, full of books)
- Post-it notes

What you do
Show the children your rucksack and invite them to try and lift it. Explain that if you were to carry this rucksack you would soon feel worn out and burdened down by it. Sometimes people talk about being 'burdened down' by bad or worrying things that are happening in their lives.

Ask the children what different emotions the slaves would have been feeling. Write each one on a Post-it note and stick it to the rucksack. Do the children ever feel like this about things that happen to them?

Invite a child to come and put the rucksack on and as they do so support the weight behind them. How does the volunteer feel? Can they walk around even though they have a heavy burden? Explain that Christians believe they can ask God for help with things that 'burden' them. He might not take the nasty things away or change what has happened, but he will give strength to cope with it – just as you are supporting the rucksack so your volunteer can cope with the weight.

This was a good visual aid to show that, with God's help, things are easier and that he wants to help us.
Theo, St Albans

The hiking equipment each week was great for recapping.
Helen, Darlington

Learn and remember
(5 minutes)

It is always good to learn Bible verses – not only do they help clarify the session's main teaching point, but they also raise the children's awareness that the Bible is a living, active message from God which can stay with them through to adulthood.

Teach the group the verse: 'Leave all your worries with him, because he cares for you. 1 Peter 5:7' (GNB). Perhaps you could do this by using actions. Hold up the fingers of one hand and use the other hand to close one finger as you say each of the first five words 'Leave all your worries with', then point up for 'him'. With one hand stroke the flat palm of the other for 'because he cares' and then point outwards for 'for you'. Make your hands into a book shape and say '1 Peter chapter 5 verse 7'.

Do the actions a couple of times whilst saying the verse, repeat it with just the actions and then say it again with no actions.

(This verse has been set to music as a downloadable song – see scriptureunion.org.uk/music.)

Travel further

⏱1 God knows how I feel

(5–10 minutes)

What you need
- Rucksack used in *Make a discovery*
- Post-it notes
- Pens or pencils

What you do
Put the rucksack down in front of the children. Remind them that God knows and cares about everything that happens *(see Learn and remember above)*.

Give out the Post-it notes and invite the children to write or draw things that are troubling them on their Post-it note and then stick it to the rucksack. When all those who want to take part have done so say a covering prayer thanking God for his care and asking for strength to cope with our burdens.

⏱2 Prayer pyramids

(15–20 minutes)

What you need
- Prayer pyramid from page 59 copied onto card for every person
- Scissors and glue
- Colouring pens or pencils

What you do
Give every child a copy of the prayer pyramid to colour and cut out. If you have limited time you could cut them out before the session. Help the children fold the card into a pyramid and glue it in place.

Remind the children that God is interested in everything that happens to them – he knows and he cares. Encourage everyone to hold their pyramid with the 'home' side facing them. Allow a short time of silence so the children can talk to God quietly about their home. Next turn the pyramids to the 'friends' side and do the same. Repeat for 'school' and 'world' and then finish with a final prayer yourself.
This idea is adapted from *New Ideas for Creative Prayer*, Scripture Union.

One girl (aged 7 or 8) was concerned because she had already prayed for her 5-year-old cousin who had cancer. Should she pray again?
Theo, St Albans

PS Make a point of personally saying 'Goodbye' to each child and if possible, speak to as many parents or carers as you can.

2

Session 2
THE BIRTH OF MOSES

Bible story: The birth of Moses (Exodus 2:1–10)

Aim: To show how God had a plan to help the Israelites and that he has a plan for our lives too.

Notes for you: In the last session the children heard how Pharaoh had forced the Israelites into slavery in order to stop any idea of rebellion. However, his plan didn't work and the nation continued to grow in strength. Pharaoh then decided to get rid of all the baby boys at birth by ordering his soldiers to throw them into the River Nile. However Pharaoh had left God out of his reckoning and he had a plan to save his people. This did not happen overnight and the Israelites needed to keep their faith through these days of darkness. It is interesting to note that, although Pharaoh had declared that baby girls would live, it is actually women who thwart his plans – the midwives, Moses' mother and sister and even his own daughter! Although the names of Moses' parents and siblings are not mentioned in these verses, Amram, Jochebed, Aaron and Miriam are named in Numbers 26:59.

Gather together

◀1 ⊕ Guess the action

(5–10 minutes)

What you need
- 10 cards with feelings written on them (for example, proud, scared, angry, lonely, bored)
- 10 cards with actions written on them (for example, open a window, bake a cake, clean your teeth, chat on the phone)

What you do
Choose a child, who enjoys acting, to pick one card from each set. They perform the action in a way that expresses the feeling. The other children guess both the feeling and the action. With a large group you could have two children performing each action. This helps children to think about their feelings.

◀2 ☺ Off to Egypt

(5 minutes plus)

What you need
- A list of words and associated actions about Egypt. These could be:
- Pyramids *(run to the left hand wall)*
- River Nile *(run to the right hand wall)*
- Palace *(run to the front)*
- Fields *(run to the back)*
- Collect straw *(bend down and pick it up)*
- Carry bricks *(carry heavy weight on shoulder)*
- Dig the ground *(pretend to dig)*
- Pharaoh *(bow and say 'Your majesty')*
- Pray to God *(kneel with hands together)*

What you do
Tell the children that they are playing the part of the slaves in Egypt. Whenever an instruction is called they have to obey and the last person

to do so is out. Run through the instructions and the different actions before you start to play 'for real'. Those children who are out could help you spot who is last to obey each time.

⊖ There was no need for anyone to be out or win because the children just enjoyed running around and joining in the actions. It also built on what they learned last week.⊝
Elis, Yealhampton

◀3 Slave and soldier

What you do
Choose one child to be the slave and another to be the soldier. All the other children form a circle and join hands. The object of the game is for the soldier to chase and catch the slave. He chases the slave around and through the circle. However, the other players are on the side of the slave and let them pass freely under their clasped hands while they try not to let the soldier through.

◀4 Make a… …basket

(15–20 minutes)

What you need
- Page 60 photocopied onto card for every child
- One strip of crêpe paper approx 1 x 200 cm long for every child
- Glue or sticky tape

What you do
Help the children to cut out their basket shape and also cut all but one of the flaps vertically in half (you need an odd number of flaps to weave). If you have time let the children decorate the centre/base of the basket. Fold

each of the flaps in towards the centre/base of the basket to make crease marks.

Attach the strip of crêpe paper to the bottom of the large flap (close to the centre of the basket). Weave the strip of paper in and out around the basket, bringing the flaps up as you go to form the sides. Keep going until you reach the top of the basket (probably about three or four circuits). Trim the crêpe paper to length and stick the end in place. You may have to add more glue around the top of the basket to keep the weave secure. As you are making the baskets, talk about the story, imagining what it would be like for Miriam, Moses, his mother and so on. If you have not yet told the story, use this activity to whet the children's appetites.

As an alternative photocopy the finger puppets (page 61–62) onto card, colour and cut them out. (See below)

Setting off

(2–5 minutes)

What you need
- Rucksack used last week (without the heavy weight!)
- Bottle of water

What you do
Show your rucksack and ask what the children remember from the last session. Although the Israelites were burdened down, God still cared for them. Either teach or remind the group of the *Learn and remember* verse: 'Leave all your worries with Jesus because he cares for you. 1 Peter 5:7' (see page 18).

Explain that when you're going on a journey there are some things you have to put into your rucksack. Show the bottle of water and ask what would happen if we didn't have anything to drink. Ask the children to look out for how water kept someone alive in the story.

Explore the Bible

⟨⟩1 Spot the mistake

(10 minutes)

What you need
- A copy of the Bible verses doctored with some obvious mistakes added. (See page 61 for suggestions based on the Contemporary English Version.)

What you do
Read the story of Moses direct from **Exodus 2:1–10**. When you have read it through once, read it again with a few obvious mistakes. When a child hears a mistake they put up their hand and tell you the correct word.

⟨⟩ The children enjoyed spotting and correcting the mistakes. ⟨⟩
Helen, Darlington

⟨⟩2 ⟨⟩Finger puppets

(10–15 minutes)

What you need
- Finger puppets from page 61–62 (you may like to enlarge them on a photocopier before making them).

What you do
Tell the story of Moses being found in the bulrushes (**Exodus 2:1–10**) whilst acting it out using the finger puppets. If the children have made some puppets as a craft activity they can copy what you do and play along. If not, choose three children to operate your puppets as Jochebed (Moses' mum), the princess and Miriam. Remember that the baby didn't have a name until the princess gave him one! The baby puppet can be slotted into Jochebed's arms, the princess' arms and the basket.

Make sure you cover all the points mentioned in the quiz!

Extra idea

This story is also found on the video *Prince of Egypt* (DreamWorks Pictures). Show the first seven minutes until the princess finds the baby, the song ends and the video fades to black. This adaptation does not mention Miriam fetching

A child's world: Children fantasise about what they will be when they 'grow up' but it is hard for them to imagine life in a year's time, let alone five/ten years! However, the truth that with God there are no accidents is not only reassuring but encourages trust and confidence in him. His plan for his Son and the salvation of the world are to be seen in this context.

2

Jochebed (her mother) to look after the baby. If you show the video you will have to make up your own quiz questions.

 Quiz

(10 minutes)

What you need
• The quiz system you prepared for the last session – see page 18

What you do
Before the children arrive, arrange the points cards on your board and cover each one with an outer card. This time you could put them in a basket shape. Divide the group into two teams and ask the questions below to each team alternately. When a child gets the answer right they choose a number from your quiz board and the outer card is removed to reveal how many points they have scored. At the end add up the points to see which team has won.

1 What had the king decided should happen to all the newborn Israelite boys? *They would be drowned*
2 When the baby was born, how long did his mother hide him for? *Three months*
3 What sort of container did she then put him in? *Basket*
4 What did she cover the basket with? *Tar*
5 Where did she put the basket with the baby inside it? *In the tall grass/reeds at the edge of the River Nile*
6 Who kept watch over the baby? *His sister, Miriam*
7 Why did the king's daughter/princess come down to the river? *For her daily swim/bathe*
8 Who did she send to get the basket? *One of her attendants/servants*
9 Who did the baby's sister (Miriam) fetch to look after the baby for the princess? *Her mother*
10 What did the princess call the baby? *Moses*

😀 *I found the quiz was a good way of recapping the story.* 😊
Dave, North Cheam

Make a discovery

(10 minutes)

What you need
• Six large strips of paper (100 cm x 10 cm) saying: great nation, own land, saved from death, learned about God, educated as an Egyptian and lived in the desert
• Glue or sticky tape

What you do
Show the children the first strip of paper saying 'great nation' and explain that hundreds of years before this story, God had promised Abraham that his descendants (family) would become a great nation. Had this promise come true? Yes – they were the Israelites. Make the strip into a circle. Show the 'own land' strip and tell the children that God had also promised Abraham that his people would have their own land. Had this promise come true? Not yet. Explain that God had a plan to save the Israelites from Pharaoh and give them their own land. Link this strip through the first one and secure it to begin to make a paper chain. Add the further links as you talk about them.

Show the 'saved from death' strip – who did God save in the story? How had God saved him? Show the 'learned about God' strip – who did Moses live with when he was small? Who would have taught him about God? Show the 'educated as an Egyptian' strip – where did Moses live when he was a bit older? In the palace he would have been educated and taught about Egypt.

Explain that when Moses was an adult he got himself into trouble with Pharaoh and had to run away from Egypt. Show the 'lived in the desert' strip. Tell the children that this was an important part of God's plan because while Moses was in the desert he learned how to survive there and what it was like. Explain that each thing that happened was a link in the chain which eventually would lead God to rescue the Israelites.

If possible, tell the children about how things have worked out in your life, and how God's plan for you has been/is being fulfilled.

Travel further

(5–10 minutes)

⏱1 Floating flowers

What you need
- A flower photocopied from page 63 for each person
- Bowl/s of water for every 6–8 children

What you do
Give everyone a flower to cut out. Ask them to write the name of someone they would like to pray for in the centre of the flower and then decorate the petals. Demonstrate how to fold the petals, one at a time, along the dotted lines, tucking the last petal under the first to secure it. Drop the flowers onto the surface of the water with the petals side up. As the children watch their own flower opening they can talk to God about the person they are remembering.

This idea is adapted from *Here's Another One I Made Earlier*, Scripture Union.

As an alternative, ask the children to write the names of people they would like to pray for on strips of paper and then join the strips up like links in a chain before saying a prayer all together.

❝ *One girl prayed for the group helpers using the floating flower.* ❞

Elis, Yealhampton

⏱2 Prayer box

(5 minutes plus)

What you need
- A decorated box with a hole in the top, labelled 'prayer box'

What you do
Give every child a piece of paper and a pen. Remind them of the *Learn and remember* verse from the last session (see page 18) which says that God cares about every part of our lives just as he was interested in and cared for Moses and his family.

Help them to write or draw a prayer to God. Perhaps this could be something they are grateful for or maybe something they are worried about (for example, maths test, broken friendship, their next school, problems at home). During a time of quiet encourage the children to put their prayers in the box, and in this way leave them with God.

You may like to write 1 Peter 5:7 on your box 'Leave all your worries with Jesus because he cares for you' and have the box available in future weeks for the children to use.

PS Make sure you personally say 'Goodbye' to each child as they leave.

3

Session 3
GOD SPEAKS TO MOSES

Bible story: God speaks to Moses at the burning bush (Exodus 3:1–15; 4:1–17,27–31)

Aim: To help the children appreciate both the talking and listening aspects of their relationship with God.

Notes for you: This session's story takes place 80 years after the incident in the bulrushes. When Moses was 40 years old he saw an Egyptian mistreating an Israelite slave, got into a fight with him and ended up killing him. When Pharaoh found out what had happened Moses ran away to Midian where he met and married Zipporah whose family were shepherds (see Exodus 2:11–25). He then spent 40 years looking after sheep in the desert before God met him on Mount Horeb (also called Sinai). Throughout Exodus fire is a symbol of God's presence – here in the burning bush and later leading the Israelites through the desert and on top of Mount Sinai whilst Moses received the Ten Commandments.

Gather together

1  Who goes there?

(5–10 minutes)

What you need
• A blindfold

What you do
Choose one child to be the 'guesser'. They are blindfolded and stand in the middle of the circle. On the command 'go' all the other children get up and change places. The guesser then points at random and asks 'Who goes there?' The child they are pointing to responds 'It's a friend from…' (add the name of your club). The blindfolded child tries to guess who is speaking. If they are correct they stay in the middle, but if they are wrong, then the two children swap roles. See who identifies the most people correctly. This helps the children to listen and speak clearly.

2 Racing whispers

(up to 10 minutes)

What you need
• Some sentences or instructions written out or illustrated clearly on separate cards (for example, spin around and clap three times, go to the front and stand on a chair).

What you do
Ask the children to line up in groups of 6–8 and spread out across your room. Make sure there is space between the teams. Show the first child in each line one of your messages or instructions. This child whispers the message to the second child in their line who whispers it to the third and so on. The last child in each line runs to you and performs the action or repeats the message.

Award points for the group who passed the message quickest and also for the group who are the most accurate. Change the first and last person with each new message.

> *This was a good illustration of the theme.*
> *Val, St Albans*

3 Burning bushes

(10 minutes)

What you do
Choose one volunteer to be the catcher and everyone else stands at one end of the hall. On the given signal the children run across the hall to safety while the catcher tries to stop them. Anyone who is tagged is set 'on fire' and becomes a burning bush. Bushes have to stay where they are; they cannot move their feet, but their arms are flames waving around. When all the children have crossed the hall they race back again while the catcher chases them. This time, however, they have to negotiate round any burning bushes. The bushes are allowed to hinder their journey but they cannot catch the other children or hold onto them.

4 Make a…
…phone

(up to 10 minutes)

What you need
• 2 disposable cups per child
• 5–6 metres of string per child
• Something to make a hole in the cup (for example bradawl)
• Sticky shapes (optional)

What you do
Give every child two disposable cups and a length of string. Help them to make a small hole

5

① 5 ⊕ Make some…
…bread

(5 minutes if only doing the last part)

BE AWARE OF FOOD ALLERGIES
If you have a small group you could make the bread with the children from scratch. However, large numbers and pressure of time might mean it's preferable to make the dough and allow it to rise before the session so the children only have to knead and shape their own piece before taking it home for baking. This recipe is enough for 12–15 children.

What you need
- 500 g strong bread flour
- 2 tsp salt
- 5 g vegetable fat
- 1 packet dried yeast
- 250 ml warm water
- Beaten egg or milk
- Plastic bags to take the dough/bread home (if not eaten during the session!)

What you do
Sieve the flour and salt into a bowl. Rub in the vegetable fat and add the dried yeast (follow manufacturer's instructions). Make a hollow in the centre of the mixture and pour in the warm water. Mix carefully and thoroughly. Turn out onto a lightly floured surface.

Flour hands and knead the dough for about ten minutes. Replace in the bowl, cover and leave to rise until it has doubled in size (approx. thirty minutes). Divide the dough between the children. Lightly flour the surface and the children's hands before they knead and shape their piece of dough for baking. Place rolls/shapes on a well-greased baking tray and leave to rise in a warm place while the oven heats up. Brush with beaten egg or milk just before baking. Bake at 220 °C, 425 °F, gas mark 7 for 20–25 minutes. Allow to cool before eating!

Setting off

(5 minutes)

What you need
- Rucksack, bottle of water, walking boots and walking pole from previous sessions
- Cagoule

What you do
Use the rucksack, water, boots and walking pole to recap what you have learned in the previous sessions. Show this session's equipment – a cagoule – and ask questions to get the idea that a cagoule protects us from rain and saves us from getting wet. So listen out for how God protects and saves the Israelites in the story.

Explore the Bible

① 1 Run for it!

(10 minutes)

What you do
Divide your children into teams and ask each team to sit in a line one behind the other. Go down the teams naming the children as different people or things mentioned in the story (for example, Moses, Pharaoh, lamb, eldest son, doorposts, midnight, bread, angel, Israelites)

As you tell the story (found in **Exodus 12**) the children listen out for their word and when they hear it they jump up, run right around their team and race back to their place. The first child back to their place scores a point for their team.

Make sure you get all the children running in the same direction or you could have some crashes in the scramble. It is also a good idea to make a note of how many times you use each word to make sure everyone has a fair go.

① 2 👓 Use a story bag

(10 minutes)

What you need
- A colourful bag
- 5 or 6 objects related to the story (for example, a toy lamb, flat [pitta] bread, family photo, sandals, a clock showing midnight, a handkerchief [for crying], jewellery)

What you do
Before the session place the objects in your story bag. As you mention the different things in the story show your objects to the children as a visual aid. If you used this method in session 1 you could liven it up by including a bogus object which you keep on bringing out by mistake. Afterwards put all the items back into your bag

A child's world: Many children will have learnt about the Jewish Passover and the role of Holy Communion. But they may not have understood its significance for them. Their understanding of Jesus' death may be even more unclear. This is a great opportunity for you to explain it as well as share what Jesus' death means to you personally. Practise carefully what you are going to say.

5

and invite the children to pull them out and tell you where they fitted in. The story is found in **Exodus 12**.

Extra idea

Although this story is featured on the *Prince of Egypt* (starting 1 hour 8.30 minutes) it emphasises the death of the firstborn son rather than the Israelites being saved through the blood. However, if you would like to use the clip, it starts with Moses instructing the Israelites about the blood and the lamb and ends when Moses returns to his home – just before the song starts. It is five minutes long.

 Quiz

(10 minutes)

What you need
- The quiz system for the first session

What you do
Before the children arrive, arrange the points cards on your board and cover each one with an outer card. Perhaps you could arrange them like a door frame. Divide the group into two teams and ask them questions alternately. When a child gets the answer right they choose a number and the outer card is removed to reveal how many points they have scored for their team.

1 What did Moses tell the king would happen because he wouldn't let the slaves go free? *God would kill the eldest son in each family*
2 What instruction did God give for the best lamb in every family? *It had to be killed*
3 What were the people to do with the lamb's blood? *Smear it on the doorposts*
4 What did they eat with their roast lamb? *Bitter herbs and bread made without yeast*
5 Tell me one special thing about the way the Israelites ate the meal. *Dressed and ready to travel, with their sandals on, standing up*
6 What is this celebration called? *Passover*
7 At what time did the angel of death 'pass over' the Hebrews' houses? *Midnight*
8 What did the king do when he called Moses and Aaron to see him? *He begged them to leave*
9 What did the Egyptians give to the Israelites? *Money, gold and silver jewellery and clothes*
10 How long had they been slaves in Egypt? *430 years*

They knew all the answers. It was good to help them understand the story.
Ross, St Albans

Make a discovery

(10 minut es)

What you need
- The letters P-A-S-S-O-V-E-R written down one side of a large piece of paper, acetate or white board

What you do
Ask the children what the festival was called that the Israelites were celebrating. Show your word written out. Explain the meaning of the Passover and as you speak fill in the words on your acrostic (see those underlined below). Don't forget to write in lower case letters as children find these easier to read.

God had made the Israelites a <u>promise</u> that he would bring them out of Egypt. Moses and Aaron went to Pharaoh to <u>ask</u> for their release but Pharaoh refused. God warned him that the eldest <u>son</u> in every family would die. God told the Israelites to <u>sacrifice</u> or kill a lamb. They had to <u>obey</u> God's instructions and paint the blood on their doorposts – otherwise the <u>verdict</u> was death. As the angel passed over the land, <u>everyone</u> who had blood on their door posts was saved. The lamb had taken the place of the Israelites and they were <u>rescued</u>.

Go back over your acrostic showing how the words relate to what Christians believe about Jesus. This is a very tight explanation of the meaning of Jesus' death. For children who are part of a church community it will be a useful summary. For unchurched children they will probably only grasp a little of it. But that is OK. Just don't try and explain everything.

God made a <u>promise</u> that he would provide a way for people who <u>ask</u> him to be forgiven, to be his friends now and live with him in heaven when they die. God sent his <u>Son</u>, Jesus into the world. Jesus never did anything wrong, but in the end he was killed or you could say made a <u>sacrifice</u> when he died on the cross. But he came alive again. No matter how hard people try, they can never <u>obey</u> God completely. This means we all do things wrong (the Bible calls this 'sin') and so the <u>verdict</u> on our lives is guilty. We deserve to be punished for what we've done wrong. But God wants <u>everyone</u> to be saved; he wants everyone to be his friend. If we say 'Sorry' to God then he will forgive us. Because of Jesus' death we can be <u>rescued</u> from not knowing God and all that that means. We can live with God in heaven forever.

> **This was a very valuable activity, which caught the children's imaginations and led to some sensible questions afterwards.**
> *Dave, North Cheam*

 Learn and remember

(5 minutes)

'Christ Jesus came into the world to save sinners. 1 Timothy 1:15' (NIV)

What you need
- An anagram for each of the words in the *Learn and remember* verse – for example,
- cirtsh / ussej / mace / tion / het / drowl / ot / vase / rinness / 1 mothyit / 15 serve 1
- Write each anagram on a separate card with the correct spelling on the back.

What you do
Show the anagrams to the group one at a time for them to work out. With a younger group you may have to simplify some of the anagrams by making the first letter of the anagram the same as the first letter of the word. Invite the child who guesses the correct word to come and hold the card with the answer showing at the front. When all the words have been guessed correctly, read the verse together; then say it again quietly; loudly; ask the boys to say it on their own; then the girls etc until the verse has been remembered.

With a small group it might be better to display the words on a board rather than have most of the children up the front holding cards and therefore unable to see what is written on them.

Alternatively, work out signs for this short verse which you can act out. Eg 'Jesus' – point to imaginary nail marks in your palms; 'world' – a globe; 'save' – pull someone up out of a hole with an imaginary rope; 'sinners' – hang and shake head.

Travel further

5

1 Jesus makes us clean

(5 minutes)

What you need
- A whiteboard or OHP and acetate
- Washable markers
- Damp cloth or kitchen roll

What you do
Show the clean whiteboard or empty acetate to the children and explain that it is clean and pure. However, it can easily be spoiled just as the wrong things we do spoil our lives and spoil our relationship with God. Ask what the Bible calls these wrong things (sins). Ask the children for ideas of sins and as each one is mentioned write it on the whiteboard. Write with big letters trying to get as many ideas as possible to completely cover the board and make it look horrible and messy. Have a time of quiet so everyone can say 'sorry' to God for the wrong they have done. After you have prayed, remind the children of the *Learn and remember* verse for this session that Jesus will forgive and save us if we ask him. Using your damp cloth or kitchen towel wipe the board so that all the writing disappears - our sins are washed away.

If you have an older group, you could give the children their own piece of acetate to write on, invite them to dampen some kitchen roll themselves and wipe the acetate clean after they have prayed.

2 Prayer wire

(5 minutes)

What you need
- Chenille wire (pipe cleaner) for everyone

What you do
Give everyone a chenille wire. Ask them to make it into the shape of a sheep – because in the story the sheep was used to save the Israelites. Change it to a cross shape because Jesus died on the cross. Finally make the shape of a tear – we can be saved because Jesus died on the cross, but only if we're sorry for the things we have done wrong and ask him to forgive us. Have a time of quiet so children can pray before you say a summary prayer.

If any children have been especially thoughtful or responsive you will want to talk further with them. Have copies of the commitment booklets (see page 12) available.

6

Session 6
CROSSING THE RED SEA

Bible story: The Israelites cross the Red Sea (Exodus 13:17–22; 14:5–31; 15:19–21)

Aim: To understand that God was with the Israelites to lead and guide them and that he will be with us too.

Notes for you: Having been set free from Egypt, the Israelites were not left to their own devices. God himself goes before them and leads them in a path they do not expect – into the wilderness (**13:17,18**). However, this was not a mistake on his part but led to a wonderful miracle and the destruction of the Egyptian army.

Gather together

◑1 Who goes with whom?

(5–10 minutes)

What you need
- Post-it notes with one half of a pair written on each (eg Posh and Becks, Ant and Dec, Winnie the Pooh and Eeyore, Batman and Robin, Shrek and Princess Fiona, Tom and Jerry)

What you do
Stick one Post-it note to everyone's forehead. Players must not see what is written on their own Post-it note. The idea is for the children to question each other to find out who they are and, once discovered, find their partner.

Questions might be: Am I real or made up? Am I male or female? Am I alive now? Am I an animal? or, if desperate, What letter does my name start with? Make sure the children realise they can't just ask 'Who am I?' This introduces the possibility of being puzzled.

◑2 Human obstacle course

(10 minutes)

What you do
Divide your children into teams, and ask each team to line up at one end of the hall. Explain that you are going to have an obstacle race and that the children themselves are the obstacles.

The first child in each team runs to the other end of the hall, touches the wall, and on their way back makes themselves into an obstacle. The second child has to negotiate this obstacle, touch the back wall and then form another obstacle. The third child now has two obstacles to negotiate and makes a third. This continues until the last child who negotiates all the

obstacles and then tags each player on their way back. This is the signal for everyone to return to the starting line. The first team back is the winner.
Obstacles might be:
Pole – child stands up straight and other children run all the way around them
Ball – child crouches down and other children jump over them
Bridge – child stands with feet apart and other children go under the bridge

◑3 ✜Triangle tag

(5 minutes)

What you do
Divide your children into groups of four. Three of the children join hands in a triangle and the fourth player stands outside the triangle. One of those in the triangle is chosen as the target. The object of the game is for the fourth player to try and tag the target while the others protect him/her by revolving the triangle and moving about. Once a target is caught the children swap roles within their group

◑4 Make a…
…windmill

(15–20 minutes)

You will need for each windmill:
- Template enlarged and photocopied from page 68 onto paper
- Garden stick or strong straw
- Pin or tack and hammer
- Small amount of plasticine

What you do
Give every child a copy of the windmill template. Ask them to decorate it on both sides and cut it out. They also need to cut the diagonal lines. Bend each of the marked corners

6

over to the centre and fix them to one end of the stick with the pin or tack (don't attach them too firmly or the windmill will not spin round when blown!). Cover the sharp end of the pin with plasticine. You can remind the children that it was a strong wind blowing all night that drove back the sea.

⑥ We used bamboo canes and drew pictures in the corner of the windmills and added beads for decoration. We then used metal bottle tops and nails to reduce the friction of the windmill. Some drilling was required, obviously under supervision. ⑤
Elis, Yealhampton

As an alternative craft idea you could make the prayer booklets (pages 70–71).

Setting off

(5 minutes)

What you need
- Walking equipment – rucksack, water, boots, pole, cagoule
- Torch

What you do
Show the children your torch and tell them that, when packing for a long walk, a torch is important – even though you might not use it. Why is this? Explain that, if you get lost or your walk takes longer than expected, it might get dark. In the countryside you won't have streetlights to show the way and you could easily stumble and fall (use a personal story to illustrate this if possible). Recap over the other items you have with you asking the children how each one reminds us of the journey along the **Rocky Road**. Ask the children to listen out for how the Israelites knew the way to go when they left Egypt.

Explore the Bible

 **Do a play**

(15 minutes)

What you need
- Three copies of page 69 with the words for Pharaoh, Moses and Miriam highlighted (each on a different sheet)
- A chair
- Two blue sheets (optional)
- One white sheet (optional)

What you do
Set up your room so you can act the story. Decide where Egypt will be and place a chair there for Pharaoh to sit on. Designate the middle of the room as the Red Sea and lay the blue sheets out on the floor. Ask for volunteers to act the parts of the cloud/angel (holding or wearing the white sheet), Pharaoh, Moses and Miriam. Give these children their own highlighted copies of the play (which is an abridged version of **Exodus 13:17 – 15:21**). The remaining children are either Egyptian soldiers or Israelites, but if you have a large group then use four children to ripple the blue sheets as the Red Sea.

Everyone starts the story in Egypt and they act their parts and read their words as you narrate and give stage directions. When it comes to the people complaining they can either repeat the words after you or simply mime their discontent whilst you read what they say. If you have time then act the story again to help the children remember it – it will be a lot quicker the second time.

⑥ We used the windmills in the story when the wind blew. ⑤
Elis, Yealhampton

⑥ Our volunteer child actors read out highlighted excerpts from the printed Bible story. It worked well. ⑤
Elis, Yealhampton

⑥2 Guess the words

(10–15 minutes)

What you need
- A large sheet of paper or white board
- A pen

A child's world:
Sometimes puzzling things happen to us. Children are often less able than an adult to make sense of things. The people of Israel were puzzled but God was with them guiding them. Some children may be facing puzzling events in their family or at school. Help them to see that this is not unusual, although unique to them, and God is with them as a guide.

6

What you do

This idea involves the children trying to guess different key words in the story.

Begin to tell the story from **Exodus 13:17 – 15:21** but before you mention the word 'desert' draw six dashes on your board (as if playing 'hangman'). Divide the children into two groups and ask them to guess alternate letters to see if they are in your word. When a letter is guessed correctly write it in the appropriate place.

However, if the chosen letter is not in the word write it somewhere else on the board (so it isn't chosen again) and also make a note of which side made the wrong guess. When the word is complete, carry on with the story. When you get to the next key word (for example, 'cloud') play again. At the end of the story the team with the fewest wrong guesses is the winner.

With younger groups, write the words out with the vowels already in place so that they only have to guess the consonants.

Possible words are: desert, cloud/fire, soldiers, complained, light/dark, dry land, drowned, tambourine.

Extra idea

The relevant excerpt from the *Prince of Egypt* is 13 minutes long. Start where you finished last time at the beginning of the song 'There can be miracles' as the people pack and then leave Egypt (1 hour 13 minutes in). Finish when Zipporah says, 'Look at your people, Moses, they are free.' Once again you will have to adapt the quiz questions.

 Quiz

(10 minutes)

What you need

- The quiz system you prepared for the first session

What you do

Before the children arrive, arrange the points cards on your board and cover each one with an outer card. Perhaps you could arrange them as waves. Divide the group into two teams and ask them questions alternately. When a child gets the answer right they choose a number which is removed to reveal how many points they have scored for their team.

1 When the people left Egypt, what did God send for them to follow? *A cloud in the day and a pillar of fire at night*

2 Why did the king change his mind and wish he hadn't let the people go? *He realised his slaves had all gone*

3 What did the people think was going to happen when they saw the king's army approaching? *They would be killed*

4 When the army caught them up, where did God's cloud move to? *Between the Israelites and Egyptians*

5 When Moses stretched his arm over the Red Sea, what did God send? *A wind*

6 How long did the wind blow for? *All night*

7 What were the people then able to do? *Walk across on dry land*

8 What happened when the Egyptians started chasing them? *Their wheels got stuck, the water came back and they drowned*

9 What musical instrument did Miriam play? *Tambourine*

10 What kind of song did they all sing? *A song of praise and victory to God*

Make a discovery

(10–15 minutes)

What you need

- Lining paper or wallpaper to represent the sea
- Paint in a tray and one or more wellington boots or paper, pencils, scissors and glue

What you do

Place the lining paper on the floor to represent the Red Sea and invite each person to put a wellington boot into the paint and make a footprint on the paper (or draw around their foot and cut it out). Write people's names on or near their footprint.

Explain that, just as God was with the Israelites on their journey, so he is with us today. Ask the children for ideas of places they go and write these on the paper in-between the footprints. Ask the children what they would do if they were worried about going to one of these places or didn't know what they should do about something (for example, if they have to have dental treatment or are facing a change of school this year). Remind them of the first two *Learn and remember* verses (see pages 18 and 26) which are reminders that God is always with them. Perhaps you could also relate back to the P-O-W-E-R prayers in session 4.

6

🔊 Learn and remember

(5 minutes)

'Be joyful always, pray continually, give thanks in all circumstances. 1 Thessalonians 5:16–18' (NIV)

What you need

- A jigsaw of the verse for groups of 5–6 children (write it out on A4 paper, photocopy it and then cut each sheet into 8–10 pieces.)

What you do

Divide the children into teams of five or six and ask them to line up at one end of your hall. Place the jigsaws at the other end, one opposite each team. The children run (relay race style) to collect the jigsaw pieces, bring them back to their team and fit them together. The first team with a completed jigsaw is the winner. Once the jigsaws are made, say the verse through together.

If you are short of space you could make the jigsaws different colours and the children could search for them in your room – or simply give them to the children to make in pairs or small groups.

🕐2 God is with us every day

(10 minutes at least)

What you need

- The template for the prayer booklets on pages 70, 71 photocopied for every person
- A sample prayer booklet

What you do

Give everyone a copy of page 71 and demonstrate how to fold and cut it into a booklet showing the days of the week. You may have to refold the pages so that 'God is with me every day' is written on the front cover. When the booklets are made, help the children to draw things or write different prayers on each day of the week.

This will take some time to complete. Either allow plenty of time in your programme, let the children take their book home to finish or allow time at the start of the next session. If you do this, you could make use of it in your prayer time in session 7.

This idea came from *New Ideas for Creative Prayer*, Scripture Union.

Travel further

🕐1 Prayer with actions

(5 minutes)

What you do

Invite the group to use both hands to point in front of them, behind them and to the sides as you say this prayer together. In the last two lines they can wrap their arms around their body and hug themselves. Try saying the prayer together once and then repeating it very quietly and again very loudly.

God goes before us
Showing us the way
God stands behind us
Helping us obey
God walks beside us
Hearing when we pray
God is always with us
Every hour of every day

🔊 This was very suitable for our group. 🔊
Val, St Albans

7

Session 7
GOD PROVIDES MANNA AND QUAIL

Bible story: God provides the Israelites with manna and quail (Exodus 16)
Aim: To realise that everything we have is given to us by God and we should thank him for it.
Notes for you: It wasn't long after the Israelites left Egypt that they began to moan to Moses with their common complaint that life was better in Egypt! This story takes the link between faith and obedience one stage further – they had to trust that God would provide manna. They also had to trust that a double portion collected would still be edible on the Sabbath day. The Israelites called the bread 'manna' which sounds like the Hebrew for 'What is it?'

Gather together

◐1 Fetch and bring

(5-10 minutes)

What you need
• A list of about 20 items which are easily found in your room or about the children's person (for example, white sock, watch, something red, someone with blue eyes, Bible, hair scrunchie).

What you do
This game is often called 'Chinese laundry'. Divide your children into teams and each team goes to a corner of the room while you stay in the middle. The teams line up. Explain that you are going to call an item from your list and the first person in the line has to fetch the item and bring it to you. One point is scored for the first team to do this. That person then goes to the back of the line and the new leader fetches the second item and so on down the list. Talk about all the different things we have on us, let alone at home or in school. We possess so much.

◐2 ⊕ ☺ A Game of toast

(5 minutes)

What you do
All the players mill around in the centre of your room. As you call out different types of bread they have to do the appropriate action. The last

child to do the action or any child who is not in a 'loaf' is out. This introduces the idea of food.
Toast – everyone jumps up and down (as in a toaster)
Roll – crouch down with hands over head
Sandwich – find a partner
Pitta – lie on the floor
French stick – greet one another saying *'Bonjour'*
Loaf with 2–8 slices – children get into groups of the specified number

> ☻ *The children were very skilled and enjoyed the Game of toast – the 'bonjour' even went well.* ☻
> *Theo, St Albans*

◐3 Snack snatching

(5 minutes)

What you need
• 'Snack' (for example, a beanbag or quoit)

What you do
Divide the children into two teams who sit facing each other. Place the 'snack' on the floor in the middle of the two teams. Number the teams from opposite ends. Call out a number and both players with that number try to snatch the 'snack' and then get back to their place without being tagged by their opposite number. Skill and cunning can be employed as players try to throw one another off the scent by making pretend grabs at the 'snack'. If a player successfully returns to their place with the 'snack', they score one point for their team. If

05 ⊕Make some…
…bread

they are tagged, then the other team scores a point. Explain that today's story is about God's people searching for their food.

◀4 ⊕Make some…
…Hannah's honey biscuits

(15 minutes plus 15 minutes cooking time)

BE AWARE OF FOOD ALLERGIES
This recipe makes about thirty biscuits. Involve as many children as possible with each stage of the recipe (creaming, adding, sifting, beating, spooning, washing up etc) as well as in shaping some of the dough into biscuits.

What you need
- 250 g (9 oz) self-raising flour
- 110 g (4 oz) butter or margarine
- 125 g (5 oz) soft brown sugar
- 1 medium egg
- 1½ tablespoons of clear honey
- 2 drops of vanilla essence

What you do
Preheat the oven to 180 °C, 350 °F, gas mark 4. Cream the butter and sugar together until soft. Add the egg and vanilla essence, then beat in the honey. Sift the flour and add it to the mixture to make a firm dough. Spoon out rounded teaspoons of the mixture and roll into balls. Slightly flatten each biscuit with your fingers. Place the biscuits on a lined baking tray about two cm apart. Bake in the centre of the oven for 12–15 minutes or until golden brown.

Extra idea

Make some fat quails using a blown-up balloon as the body with fan-folded paper for the tail and wings. Two identical pieces of folded card stuck together can form a beak. Attach everything to the quail's body using sticky tape.
For an alternative craft idea make the paper plate prayers (page 43).

Setting off

(5 minutes)

What you need
- A packed lunch

What you do
Tell the children that you haven't had anything to eat for ages but it's OK because your friend has given you a packed lunch. Open your lunch and begin complaining about it – you don't like ham – only cheese sandwiches; it's the wrong flavour crisps; the apple looks old etc. In the end discard your lunch and say you'd be better off starving to death.
Have you ever wondered what the Israelites ate in the desert? Certainly not SANDwiches!!

⑤ *This was very good – the children enjoyed telling me off for not liking my food!* ⑨
Susan, North Cheam

Explore the Bible

◀1 ☺Join in with actions

(10 minutes)

What you need
A copy of the verses on page 72 (optional)

What you do
Explain to the children that they need to listen carefully as you tell the story because every time they hear certain words they need to do a different action. Tell the children what those words are (see below) and demonstrate the actions. Let the children practise. Either read the abridged version of the Bible story from page 72 or tell it in your own words (see **Exodus 16**) making sure you include the words below a number of times each. You will need to explain what the Sabbath was.
Desert – wipe hand across forehead
Bread – rub tummy
Meat – pretend to eat
Morning – yawn and stretch
Gather/gathered – a sweeping movement with your arm
Worms – wiggle first finger

⑤ *One girl had actually eaten quail meat!* ⑨
Theo, St Albans

A child's world:
Children possess so much these days in the west, and even if they don't, children they know or see on television own a wealth of games, toys, clothes etc. To trust God to provide for us is a difficult concept to grasp. Encouraging the children to be thankful to God for all he has given them is very much part of what it means to be in relationship with him. Being content is connected to this.

7

2 Conduct an interview

(10 minutes)

What you need

- Clipboard with questions/prompts to help your interview
- Microphone (optional)
- Costumes for an Israelite and an interviewer (optional)

What you do

Before the session starts, ask another leader to help you by taking the part of an Israelite while you are a reporter. Set the scene by telling the children that you are in the desert and have heard some strange things about people who are living there in tents. 'Happen' to see an Israelite and ask if they will answer a few questions for you. Conduct your interview making sure that your interviewee covers the main points of the story.

Questions might include: What nation do you belong to? How long have you lived in the desert? Where did you live before? What was it like living there? How are you managing to survive? What are you eating? Where does this stuff come from? What does it taste like?

3 Quiz

(10 minutes)

What you need

- The quiz system you prepared for the first session

What you do

Before the children arrive, arrange the points cards on your board and cover each one with an outer card. Perhaps you could arrange them to look like a bucket. Divide the group into two teams and ask them questions alternately. When a child gets the answer right they choose a number which is removed to reveal how many points they have scored for their team.

1   Where were the Israelites camping? *In the desert*
2   What were the Israelites complaining about? *They thought they would starve*
3   What type of bird did God send to the camp? *Quail*
4   What time of day did the manna come? *Morning*
5   What colour was the manna? *White*

6   How much manna did they have to collect for each person? *2 litres*
7   What did the manna taste like? *Wafers made with honey*
8   What happened to any manna which was kept until the next day? *It was stinking and full of worms*
9   Why did they have to gather twice as much on the day before the Sabbath? *Because there wouldn't be any the next day*
10 What was the saved manna like on the Sabbath day? *It was fine and OK to eat*

Make a discovery

(10 minutes)

What you need

- Eight large (A4) cards with one of each of the following letters written on the back: THANKYOU

What you do

Ask the children to think of things that they (or other people) complain about. Quickly draw (or write) each idea on one of your cards and invite the child who suggested it to come and hold that card at the front so the picture shows (ideas might include weather, clothes, food, money, homework, TV programmes, chores, bedtime). If you have a small group, display the cards on a board where everyone can see them, rather than most of the children standing at the front.

When all your cards have been used, briefly go through each thing and think of reasons why we shouldn't complain about them but instead be thankful. Invite the children to turn their cards around to show the words 'thank you'. Make the point that we have so much and are so blessed that we should spend more time thanking people (including God) than moaning and groaning. The Israelites had much to thank God for too – but they ended up moaning to Moses about the lack of food.

Remind the group of last session's *Learn and remember* verse (see page 39 if you want to teach it): 'Be joyful always, pray continually, give thanks in all circumstances. 1 Thessalonians 5:16–18.' Whatever happens to us we should always pray and give thanks!

Travel further

 Paper plate prayers

(5–10 minutes)

What you need
- Paper plate for every child
- Pictures of food from magazines (optional)

What you do
Give every child a paper plate and ask them to write a prayer in the centre thanking God for their food. Afterwards they can draw their favourite food on the plate or decorate it with pictures cut from magazines. Once the plates have been decorated, sit in a circle and let the children take turns to read out their prayer of thanks to God.

2 Teaspoon prayers

(5 minutes)

What you need
- A teaspoon (possibly one for everybody)

What you do
Show the children your teaspoon and ask what it is. If you made biscuits during the session refer back to the recipe as you explain that the abbreviation in recipes for teaspoon is 'tsp'. Explain that a teaspoon can help us remember how to pray to God.
T – stands for thank you
S – stands for sorry
P – stands for please
Ask for ideas of what we can say thank you, sorry or please for and then say a covering prayer including the children's ideas (or give them the opportunity to speak out their own prayers to God). Give out the teaspoons to every child to help them remember how to pray (optional) and remind them of the *Learn and remember* verse (see page 42).

God led the Hebrews from Egypt-land
Across the desert, over the sand.
He told them, 'I will care for you
If you follow me in all you do.'

We will obey, we'll do what you say.
We'll keep your laws and start today.

Moses climbed Mount Sinai.
No one followed or they would die.
They heard a trumpet long and loud –
God had come down in fire and cloud.

The people stood and shook with fear.
Then God spoke and they all could hear,
'I alone your God will be.
Do not worship any god but me.

'Don't make idols from gold or wood.
Use my name the way you should.
One day a week you must keep free,
Instead of work you worship me.

'Respect your parents – Mum and Dad.
Do not murder – that makes me sad.
Always be faithful to your husband or wife.
Keep my laws and live a good life.

'Do not take what is not yours.
Speak the truth, these are my laws.
If someone's got something you wish you had,
Don't be jealous cos envy is bad.'

This poem is for Session 8 *Explore the Bible*

7

43

8

Session 8
GOD GIVES LAWS TO HIS PEOPLE

Bible story: The Ten Commandments are given to Moses (Exodus 19; 20:1–17)

Aim: To show that God knows the best way for people to live and so we should keep his laws

Notes for you: After the Israelites left Egypt, God made a covenant (promise) with the people. He said that if they kept his laws then they would be his chosen nation and treasured possession forever – the people readily agreed and then straight away disobeyed (see Exodus 32 next session). The first four commandments deal with people's attitude to God, and the final six with their relationships with others. Israel remained camped at the foot of Mount Sinai from Exodus 19:1 until the end of the book (a period of about a year).

Gather together

◖◗1 😐 Match the rules

(10 minutes)

What you need
- An answer sheet with the first half of each rule written on it
- The second half of each rule written on a separate card and stuck up around your room

What you do
Give everyone an answer sheet and pencil. They have to complete the rules on their sheet by matching them with the endings stuck up around the room (Warning: some of the rules make sense even if they are wrong). At the end go through the answers to find the winner. Talk about what rules are for.

No / diving at any time
Please keep / off the grass
Eat five pieces of fruit / or vegetables every day
Silence / in the library
Parking allowed / for one hour only
Please switch off / mobile phones
Put your litter / in the bin
Queue / here
Stop / at the red light
No more than eight people / in this lift

> 🙂 *We did Match the rules on a flip chart and it went very well.* 🙂
> *Ross, St Albans*

> 🙂 *I got a row of kids to hold the beginnings and stand down one side of the room and another row to stand down the other side. Then they had to find their partner. Of course some*

of the words could go with other halves so it was good fun sorting them out.* 🙂
Chris, North Cheam

◖◗2 😐 Do as I say, not as I do

(5 minutes)

What you do
Play an adaptation of the game 'Simon says...' One person is the leader. They tell the children to do something (for example, put your hands on your head, jump up and down, touch your toes, reach to the sides, clap three times) while they themselves do the opposite (for example, hands on their knees, crouch down, stretch high, fold their arms, stamp three times). The children have to obey what the leader has said, and ignore what the leader has done. Talk about why you might obey someone and the importance of practising what you preach!

◖◗3 😐 Rule of the game

(5–10 minutes)

What you do
Ask one or more children to leave the room while the others decide on a rule for the game. On their return the child begins to ask simple random questions to different children (for example, What day is it? What is your name? Where do you live?). The children must answer according to the rule. The child has to guess what rule everyone is obeying and, once it is guessed, the game is repeated with a different child/rule.
Possible rules might be:
Sit with your arms folded

Before you answer you must cough
Scratch your head whilst answering
Start your answer with the words 'sometimes'
Whisper your answer
Use the word 'amazing' in your answer

▶4 😎 Remote control

(5–10 minutes)

What you do
Tell the children to imagine you have a remote control from a CD or video player. As you press the different buttons they move round the room according to your instructions. This introduces the need to obey an instruction.
Play – walk forwards
Fast Forward – run on the spot
Rewind – walk backwards
Pause – stand still (freeze)
Search – walk forwards in slow motion
Stop – sit down

> 🙂 *This was just what we needed to start the session off – some running around and simple instructions.* 🙂
>
> *Elis, Yealhampton*

▶5 ⊕ Make a...
...game of Pick-up-sticks

(10 minutes to make plus playing time)

What you need
- 25 kebab sticks for each child
- Colouring pens
- Scrap paper

What you do
Each child divides their sticks into four groups of six with one left over. This leftover stick is the pick-up-stick and they colour it all one colour. The children then colour 2 to 3 cm at each end of all the other sticks – using a different colour for each of the four groups. The colouring is easier if the children rest on scrap paper so they don't have to be too neat.

If you are unhappy about using pointed kebab sticks cut the pointed end off with a craft knife (the 'pick-up-stick' will still need a point though).

To play
Talk about the importance of rules as you prepare to play this.

One player picks up the 24 sticks and throws them onto the play area. S/he then uses the pick-up-stick to try and pick up each stick individually without moving any of the others. Once a stick has been flicked away so it is no longer touching any others it can be picked up by hand. If the player does nudge another stick, his/her turn is over and the next player picks up the remaining bundle and throws again. When all the sticks have been picked up the player who has picked up the most sticks is the winner. An alternative game can be played with players picking up only one colour of stick and seeing who manages to collect all their sticks first. Or play solo by attempting to beat your record each time you play.

Setting off

(10 minutes)

What you need
- All your walking equipment inside the rucksack (including last session's packed lunch)
- Guidebook

What you do
Show the rucksack and ask how it reminds you of God and the Israelites. Ask the children what other equipment you have collected and, as they mention the different things, take them out of your rucksack and talk about the different stories you have had so far.

Tell them that you now have loads of equipment but there is something missing – you don't know where you are going or how to get there. What do you need? Produce the guidebook from the rucksack. Read out a paragraph from the book and explain that without this you will easily get lost and go the wrong way.

Explain that in this session's story God told the Israelites what their guidelines should be.

> 🙂 *It amazes me how the children remember all the walking equipment every week – even if we forget something!* 🙂
>
> *Fiona, North Cheam*

A child's world:
Children know all about rules – at school, in sport – and they do know that rules are needed for the smooth running of any community. God's rules were created for the well-being of his people, evidence of his grace. We cannot win his favour by keeping his rules and being good! It is an immensely freeing thing for children (and adults) to grasp this! Think about how you would explain this to the children in your club.

8

Explore the Bible

 Rhythm and rhyme

(10 minutes)

What you need
- A good sense of rhythm!
- The rhyme on page 43

What you do
Devise a simple 4-beat rhythm which the children can join in (for example, slap knees, clap, click, click). Demonstrate how to fit the chorus to the rhythm and let the children practise it. When they have mastered the chorus, perform the whole chant, with you saying the verses and the children joining in with the chorus.

> *I thought Rhythm and rhyme looked interesting and it worked well because the kids were joining in rather than talking or fiddling about.*
>
> Elis, Yealhampton

2 Tell the story with sound effects

(10 minutes)

What you need
- The abridged version of **Exodus 19,20** taken from the CEV (see page 73). Devise different actions and sound effects as you read the story, which another leader can do and the children imitate. Keep the sound going (maybe quietly) until the next sound is introduced. For example, Moses tramping, whooshing cloud/smoke sound, washing clothes, snatch back a finger as though burnt, trumpet sound, thunder, lightning, hold up fingers for numbers of the commandments.

3 Quiz

(10 minutes)

What you need
- The quiz system you prepared for the first session

What you do
Before the children arrive, arrange the points cards on your board and cover each one with an outer card. Perhaps you could arrange them as two stone tablets. Divide the group into two teams and ask them questions alternately. When a child gets the answer right they choose a number which is removed to reveal how many points they have scored for their team.

1   Which mountain did Moses climb to meet with God? *Mount Sinai*
2   What did God tell Moses the people would be if they obeyed him? *His very own people, a holy nation*
3   What did God say would happen to anyone who touched the mountain? *They would die*
4   On the third day God came down on the mountain – what did he come down in? *Fire*
5   What noise did the people hear? *Thunder and a loud trumpet blast*
6   How did the fire, smoke, thunder, lightning, trumpet blast and earthquake make the people feel? *Scared*
7   Who heard God giving the commandments? *Everyone*
8   What were three of the commandments God gave to the people? *Only worship God, don't make idols, don't swear, remember the Sabbath Day, respect your parents, do not murder, be faithful in marriage, do not steal, do not lie, do not be jealous*
9   Name another two of the commandments. *(See above)*
10 What did the people promise they would do? *Everything God had commanded*

Make a discovery

(10 minutes)

What you need
- A disc with the word GOD written on it

What you do
Place the disc on the floor and invite everyone to stand around it in a close circle. Explain that when the people received the Ten Commandments they were close to God – they were his friends and had heard his voice speaking. However, it didn't take long for the people to disobey God and break his commandments. Explain that it wasn't just the Israelites who broke God's laws – we do it too!

When we break God's laws our friendship with God gets broken. Read the list of the commandments from page 73 starting with number 10 (Do not be jealous) and working backwards to number 1. Tell the children that every time you mention a commandment they have broken, they should take a step away from the central disc. Leaders need to join in as well. You may need to expand on some of the rules or include other things like saying or thinking 'I wish you were dead' for commandment 6.

Ask the children if they know what the Bible calls it when we disobey God? Sin. God knows we can't keep his rules on our own and so he has given us someone to help us keep them and forgives us when we do break his rules. Who is this person? Recap the *Learn and remember* verse from session 5 (page 35) – 'Christ Jesus came into the world to save sinners. 1 Timothy 1:15.' Explain that if we ask Jesus to forgive us then he will and we can be friends with God again. Shout 'Jesus' and everyone can run back to the centre to stand close around the circle.

⊘ Learn and remember

(5 minutes)

'Love the LORD your God with all your heart, with all your soul and with all your strength. Deuteronomy 6:5' (GNB)
This verse is available as a downloadable song on www.scriptureunion.org.uk/music.

What you need
- Each word (and the reference) written on a separate card
- Blu-tack

What you do
Hide the cards around your room and invite the children to go and find them. When the cards are found they should be brought to you and stuck onto a board. Rearrange the cards so they are in the correct order and then say the verse together. Remove four cards and say the verse again (filling in the gaps). Remove four more cards and repeat. Continue until the whole verse can be said with no prompts at all.

Travel further

⊙1 Road sign prayers

(5 minutes)

What you need
- Copies of four road signs downloaded from the Internet or copied from the Highway Code, enlarged so everyone can see them. (For example, school patrol (people at school); tunnel (people whose life is sad/dark, through illness or bereavement); slippery road (people who are worried about something); no footpath - adult and child holding hands (our families)

What you do
Explain that there are lots of places where we have rules – home, school, games and rules of the road. Show the road signs and explain that you are going to use them to help you think about different people and pray for them. Show the different signs and invite the children to say their prayers out loud for each area – or prime another leader to pray each time.

⊙2 Sand prayers

(5 minutes)

What you need
- A tray with some sand in it

What you do
Show the children your tray and explain that as the Israelites were in the desert they would have seen lots of sand! God gave the people some laws so that they could live the best way but it's very easy to break God's laws. What might we do or say to break one of God's laws? Use your finger or invite the children to write things like 'lie' 'cheat' 'steal' 'hurt' in the sand. Say a prayer saying sorry to God for the times when we have done these things. When you have finished the prayer, gently shake your tray to make the writing disappear – God has forgiven us for the wrong things we have done and they have gone away.

Again you can recap the *Learn and remember* verse from session 5 (page 35).

9

Session 9
THE GOLDEN CALF

Bible story: Aaron builds a golden calf and the people worship it (Exodus 32)

Aim: To recognise how easy it is to put other things before God. God is living and active; we should put him first and worship him.

Notes for you: In the last story the Israelites promised to follow God and keep his rules. Here they are, just a few weeks later, building a golden calf and declaring that it is sovereign and brought them out of Egypt. Much of the gold used in the calf would have come from the Egyptians themselves (12:35,36). The reason for the calf was probably simply boredom – Moses had been up the mountain with Joshua for a long time and they were fed up. However, Aaron's lack of leadership and ease of being persuaded by the people cannot be ignored. How true is the old adage 'The devil finds work for idle hands to do'.

Gather together

◑1 ✦Laughing statues

(5 minutes)

What you do
Invite the children to find a partner. One child in each pair is the statue. They adopt a position and have to keep still while their partner does their best to make them laugh. Once a child laughs they swap roles. At the end ask for nominations of those who made excellent statues and invite them to the front while you try to make them laugh. You could talk about statues that are famous or are familiar in your community.

> ☺ *This was a fun way to start the session – once they worked out that they weren't both being statues at the same time!* ☺
> *Elis, Yealhampton*

◑2 ☺Pin the tail on the calf

(5–10 minutes)

What you need
• A large picture of a calf without a tail (photocopied and enlarged from page 77)
• A blindfold
• A separate tail with Blu-tack attached (A large group would need more than one calf.)

What you do
Display your picture of a calf at a reachable height. One by one invite the children to be blindfolded and attach the tail where they think it should go. After each turn, mark the position with the child's initials. Don't forget to let them see where they have put the tail before

removing it for the next child's turn. The winner is the child who manages to position their tail closest to the correct position. This prepares children for the story of the golden calf.

> ☺ *We enjoyed this – a good party game for little ones so they were familiar with the concept.* ☺
> *Elis, Yealhampton*

◑3 Head it/catch it

(5–10 minutes)

What you need
• A soft/sponge ball

What you do
Ask the children to stand in a circle while you stand in the middle. Explain that you are going to throw the ball to the children individually and will tell them to either 'head it' or 'catch it'. However, whatever instruction you give them they must do the opposite. With older groups invite children who succeed to swap with you in the middle. The importance of listening to what you are told and deciding whether to obey or not should become apparent.

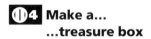

◑4 Make a...
...treasure box

(15–20 minutes)

What you need
• Page 74 photocopied onto card for every child
• Gold/silver/jewels to decorate the box (eg foil)
• Coloured pens
• Glue and scissors
• Sweets to go in the boxes (optional)

What you do
Give out the boxes so the children can colour or decorate the four sides and the lid. Cut it out.

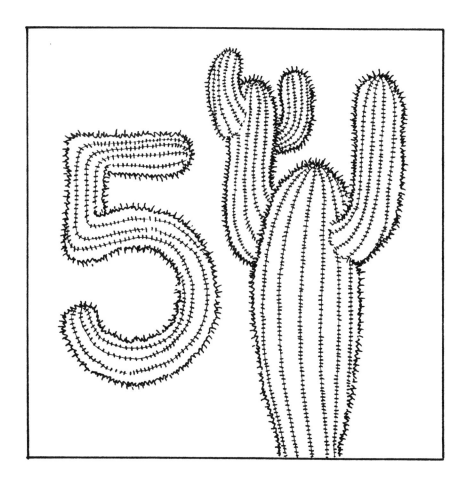

Number 10 is on page 63

Session 1

Prayer pyramid

Copy this pyramid for every child. Colour the pyramid, cut it out, fold inwards along the dotted lines and glue where indicated.

Adapted from *New Ideas for Creative Prayer* (Scripture Union) page 62 and used with permission.

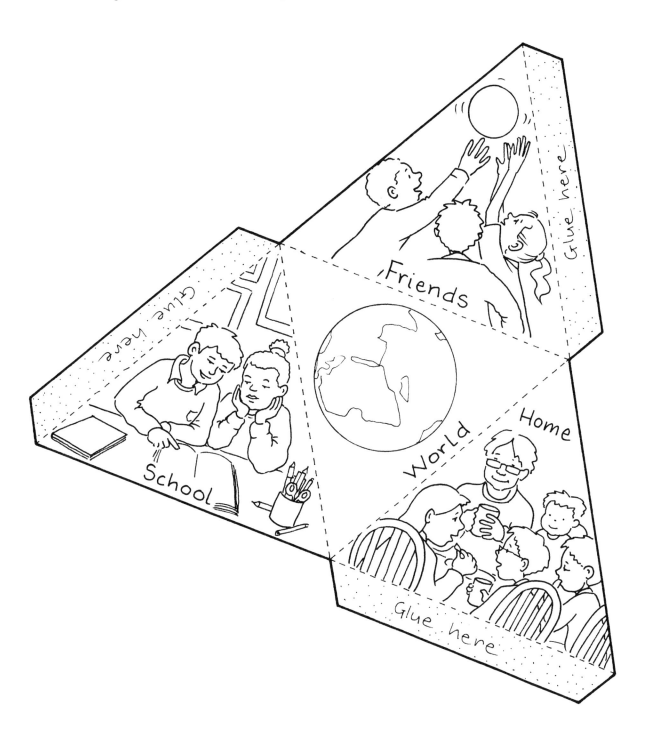

2

Session 2
Basket craft

You will need the page photocopied onto card for every child plus one strip of crêpe paper approximately 1 x 200 cm long for every child, glue or sticky tape.

Cut out the basket shape and also cut all but one of the flaps vertically in half (you need an odd number of flaps to weave). Decorate the centre/base of the basket. Fold each of the flaps in towards the centre to make crease marks. Attach the strip of crêpe paper to the bottom of the large flap (is close to the centre of the basket). Weave the strip of paper in and out around the basket, bringing the flaps up as you go to form the sides. (You may need to add glue to the occasional flap to help hold the basket together.) Keep going until you reach the top of the basket (probably about 3 or 4 circuits). Trim the crêpe paper to length and glue the end in place. You may have to add more glue around the top of the basket to keep the weave secure.

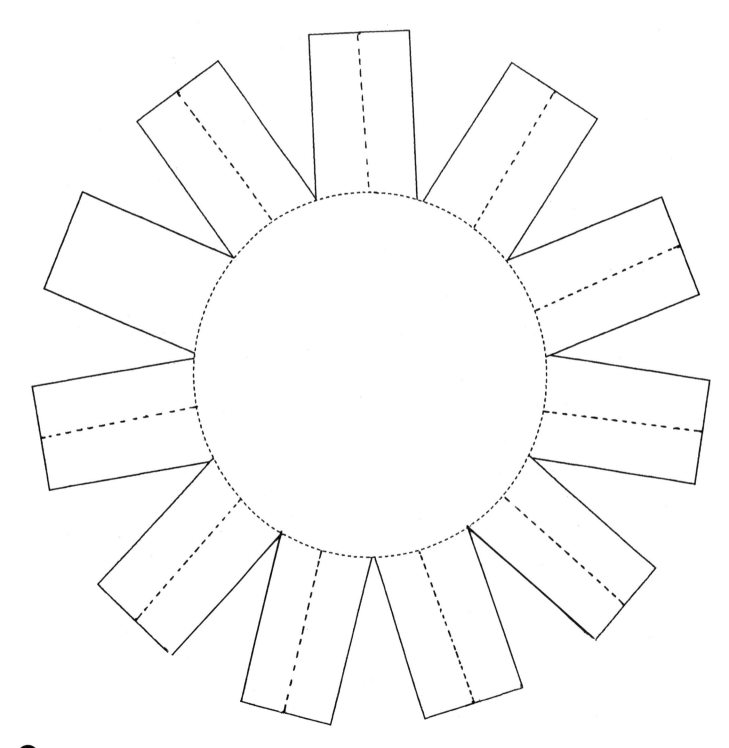

**Session 2
Exodus 2:1–10**

Read this story (taken from the Contemporary English Version) through once correctly and then again with the mistakes in brackets. The children spot the mistakes and tell you what the correct word should be.

A man from the Levi tribe married a woman from the same tribe, and she later had a baby boy (girl). He was a beautiful child, and she kept him inside for three (seven) months. But when she could no longer keep him hidden, she made a basket (table) out of reeds and covered it with tar. She put him in the basket and placed it in the tall (short) grass along the edge of the River Nile. The baby's older sister (brother) stood at a distance to see what would happen to him.

About that time one of the king's daughters (soldiers) came down to take a bath in the river, while her servant women walked along the river bank (road). She saw the basket in the tall grass and sent one of the young women to pull it out of the water (hole). When the king's daughter opened the basket, she saw the baby (kitten) and felt sorry for him because he was crying (sleeping). She said, 'This must be one of the Hebrew babies.'

At once the baby's older sister came up and asked, 'Do you want me to get a Hebrew woman to take care (a photograph) of the baby for you?'

'Yes,' the king's daughter answered.

So the girl brought the baby's mother (auntie), and the king's daughter told her, 'Take care of this child, and I will pay (punish) you.'

The baby's mother carried him home (to hospital) and took care of him. And when he was old enough, she took him to the king's daughter, who adopted (played with) him. She named him Moses (Michael) because she said, 'I pulled him out of the water.'

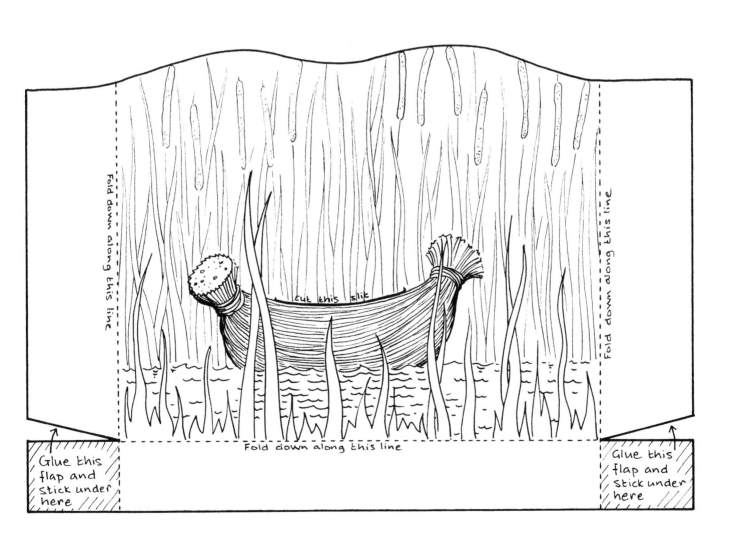

2

**Session 2
Finger puppets**

Photocopy onto card, colour and cut to use
when telling the story.

2

Session 2
Floating flowers

Instructions:
Give every child a flower to cut out. Ask them to write their own name or the name of someone they want to pray for in the centre of the flower and then decorate the petals. Fold the flowers lightly and tuck the last petal under the first to secure it. Drop the flowers onto the surface of the water with the petals on top. As the children watch their own flower slowly opening up they can say their own silent prayer asking for God's help.

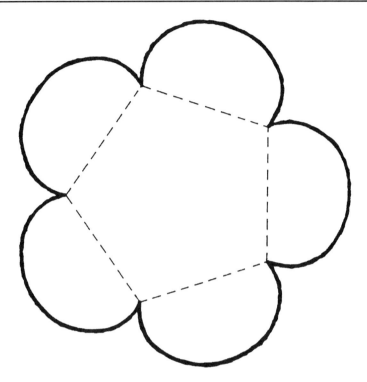

For use with the Quiz

3

Session 3
God speaks to Moses

Exodus 3:1–8a,10–12a,13b–15; 4:1–7,10-17 (CEV)

Narrator: One day, Moses was taking care of the sheep and goats of his father-in-law Jethro, the priest of Midian, and Moses decided to lead them across the desert to Sinai, the holy mountain. There an angel of the LORD appeared to him from a burning bush. Moses saw that the bush was on fire, but it was not burning up.

Moses: This is strange! I'll go over and see why the bush isn't burning up.

Narrator: When the LORD saw Moses coming near the bush, he called him by name

God: Moses! Moses!

Moses: Here I am.

God: Don't come any closer. Take off your sandals – the ground where you are standing is holy.

Narrator: Moses was afraid to look at God, and so he hid his face.

God: I have seen how my people are suffering as slaves in Egypt, and I have heard them beg for my help because of the way they are being ill-treated. I feel sorry for them, and I have come down to rescue them from the Egyptians. I will bring my people out of Egypt into a country where there is good land, rich with milk and honey. Now go to the king! I am sending you to lead my people out of his country.

Moses: Who am I to go to the king and lead your people out of Egypt?

God: I will be with you.

Moses: But what should I say, if they ask me your name?

God: I am the eternal God. So tell them that the LORD, whose name is 'I Am', has sent you. This is my name for ever, and it is the name that people must use from now on.

Moses: Suppose everyone refuses to listen to my message, and no one believes that you really appeared to me?

God: What's that in your hand?

Moses: A walking stick.

God: Throw it down!

Narrator: So Moses threw the stick on the ground. It immediately turned into a snake, and Moses jumped back.

God: Pick it up by the tail!

Narrator: When Moses did this, the snake turned back into a walking stick.

God: Put your hand inside your shirt.

Narrator: Moses obeyed, and when he took it out, his hand had turned as white as snow – like someone with leprosy.

God: Put your hand back inside your shirt.

Narrator: Moses did so, and when he took it out again, it was as healthy as the rest of his body.

God: Do this, and the Israelites will believe that you have seen me, the God who was worshipped by their ancestors Abraham, Isaac, and Jacob.

Moses: I have never been a good speaker. I wasn't one before you spoke to me, and I'm not one now. I am slow at speaking, and I can never think of what to say.

God: Who makes people able to speak or makes them deaf or unable to speak? Who gives them sight or makes them blind? Don't you know that I am the one who does these things? Now go! When you speak, I will be with you and give you the words to say.

Moses: LORD, please send someone else to do it.

Narrator: The LORD became irritated with Moses.

God: What about your brother Aaron, the Levite? I know he is a good speaker. He is already on his way here to visit you, and he will be happy to see you again. Aaron will speak to the people for you, and you will be like me, telling Aaron what to say. I will be with both of you as you speak, and I will tell each of you what to do. Now take this walking stick and use it to perform miracles.

Session 3

Photocopy onto acetate or onto card, colour
and cut to use with *Make a discovery*.

4

Session 4

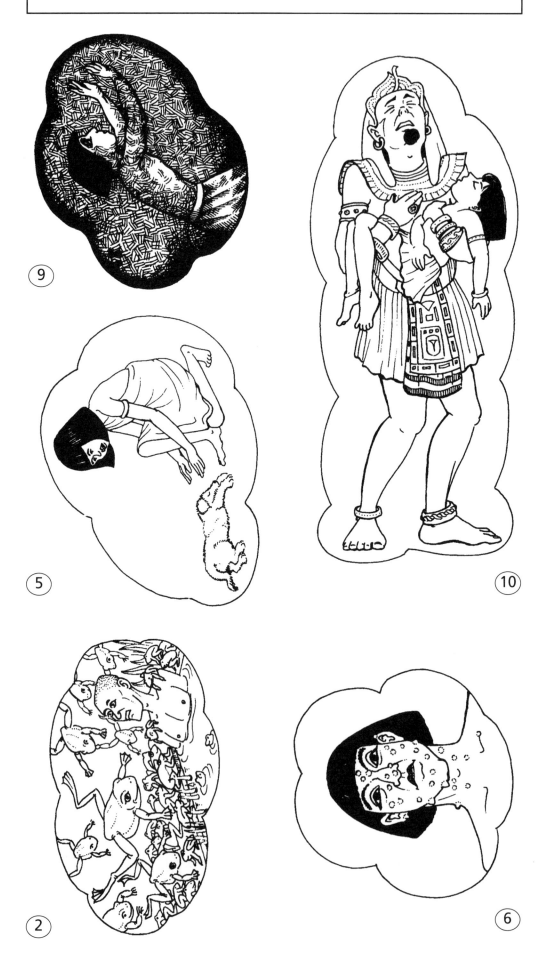

Session 4

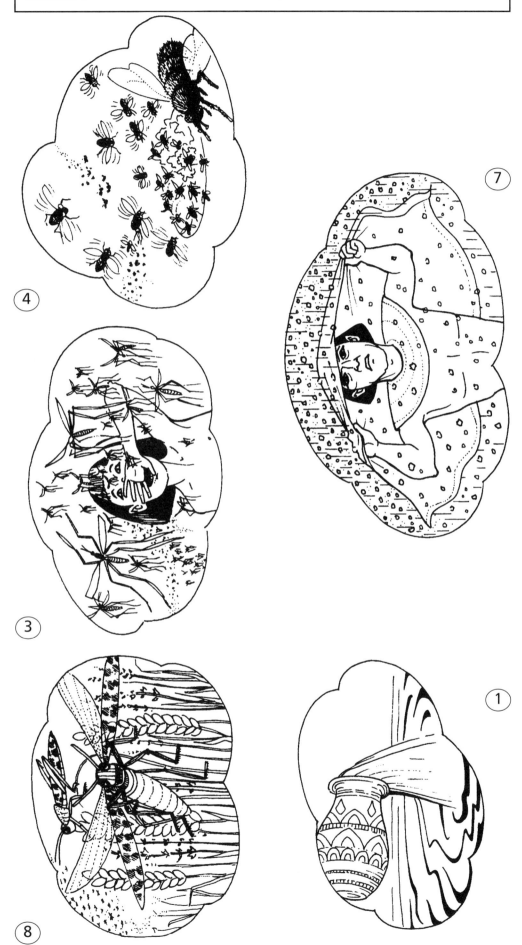

6

Session 6
Windmill craft template

Photcopy and enlarge

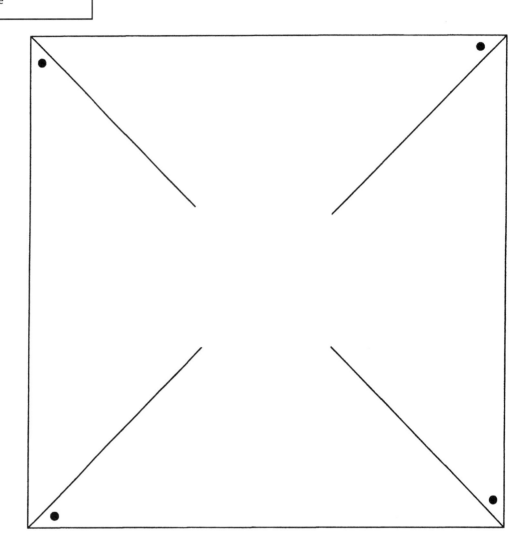

Session 4
A door hanger

Photcopy and enlarge

Session 6
Crossing the Red Sea

Exodus 13:17a,18a 21,–22;
14:5–7,9–11,13–14,19–28; 15:20–21
(CEV)

Narrator: After the king had finally let the people go, the LORD led them around through the desert and towards the Red Sea. During the day the LORD went ahead of his people in a thick cloud, and during the night he went ahead of them in a flaming fire. That way the LORD could lead them at all times, whether day or night. When the king of Egypt heard that the Israelites had finally left, he and his officials changed their minds.

Pharaoh: Look what we have done! We let them get away, and they will no longer be our slaves.

Narrator: The king got his war chariot and army ready. He commanded his officers in charge of his six hundred best chariots and all his other chariots to start after the Israelites. The king's horses and chariots and soldiers caught up with them while they were camping by the Red Sea. When the Israelites saw the king coming with his army, they were frightened and begged the LORD for help. They also complained to Moses.

People: Wasn't there enough room in Egypt to bury us? Is that why you brought us out here to die in the desert? Why did you bring us out of Egypt anyway?

Moses: Don't be afraid! Be brave, and you will see the LORD save you today. These Egyptians will never bother you again. The LORD will fight for you, and you won't have to do a thing.

Narrator: All this time God's angel had gone ahead of Israel's army, but now he moved behind them. A large cloud had also gone ahead of them, but now it moved between the Egyptians and the Israelites. The cloud gave light to the Israelites, but made it dark for the Egyptians, and during the night they could not come any closer.

Moses stretched his arm over the sea, and the LORD sent a strong east wind that blew all night until there was dry land where the water had been. The sea opened up, and the Israelites walked through on dry land with a wall of water on each side.

The Egyptian chariots and cavalry went after them. But before daylight the LORD looked down at the Egyptian army from the fiery cloud and made them panic. Their chariot wheels got stuck, and it was hard for them to move.

Egyptians: Let's leave these people alone! The LORD is on their side and is fighting against us.

God: Stretch your arm towards the sea – the water will cover the Egyptians and their cavalry and chariots.

Narrator: Moses stretched out his arm, and at daybreak the water rushed towards the Egyptians. They tried to run away, but the LORD drowned them in the sea. The water came and covered the chariots, the cavalry, and the whole Egyptian army that had followed the Israelites into the sea. Not one of them was left alive. Miriam the sister of Aaron was a prophet. So she took her tambourine and led the other women out to play their tambourines and to dance.

Miriam: Sing praises to the LORD for his great victory! He has thrown the horses and their riders into the sea.

6

Session 6
Prayer booklet

① Take a piece of A4 paper and fold the length in half from right to left. ⇒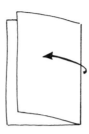

② Fold it in half from top to bottom and then unfold it again. ⇒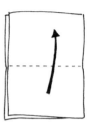

③ Fold it in half from right to left and then unfold it again. ⇒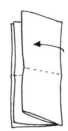

④ You should have fold lines in the shape of a cross. Cut along the right hand crease from the folded side into the middle. ⇒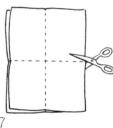

⑤ Open out the paper. ⇒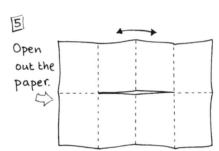

⑥ Fold the length in half from top to bottom. ⇒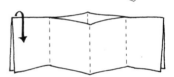

⑦ Push the two sides together, so the middle section folds outwards.

⑧ Push the pages round to make the booklet.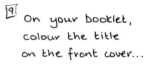

⑨ On your booklet, colour the title on the front cover...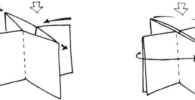

... and draw or stick appropriate pictures on the seven remaining sides.

---

1 Photocopy page 71 for each child and fold the length in half from right to left to make it A5 in size.
2 Fold it in half from top to bottom and then unfold it again. (Do not unfold your original fold.)
3 Fold it in half from right to left and then unfold it again.
4 You should have an A5 piece of paper with fold lines in the shape of a cross. Cut along the right hand crease from the fold side into the middle.

5 Open out the whole paper.
6 Fold the length in half from top to bottom.
7 Hold the paper as shown and push the two sides together, so that the middle section folds outwards.
8 Push the two sides together to make the middle pages of the book.
9 You now have a simple booklet. Write a title on the front cover and draw or stick appropriate pictures on the seven remaining sides.

Sunday

Saturday

cut through both thicknesses

God
is with
me
every
day

Friday

Monday

Thursday

Tuesday

Wednesday

7

Session 7
God provides manna and quail

Exodus 16:1–3, 9–27, 31, 35–36 (CEV)

Read the story below, and whenever you come to one of the emboldened words the children join in with an appropriate action.
Desert – wipe hand across forehead
Bread – rub tummy
Meat – pretend to eat
Morning – yawn and stretch
Gather/gathered – a sweeping movement with your arm
Worms – wiggle finger

On the fifteenth day of the second month after the Israelites had escaped from Egypt, they left Elim and started through the western edge of the Sinai **Desert** in the direction of Mount Sinai. There in the **desert** they started complaining to Moses and Aaron, 'We wish the Lord had killed us in Egypt. When we lived there, we could at least sit down and eat all the **bread** and **meat** we wanted. But you have brought us out here into this **desert**, where we are going to starve.'

Moses turned to Aaron and said, 'Bring the people together, because the Lord has heard their complaints.'

Aaron was speaking to them, when everyone looked out towards the **desert** and saw the bright glory of the Lord in a cloud. The Lord said to Moses, 'I have heard my people complain. Now tell them that each evening they will have **meat** and each **morning** they will have more than enough **bread**. Then they will know that I am the Lord their God.'

That evening a lot of quails came and landed everywhere in the camp, and the next **morning** dew covered the ground. After the dew had gone, the **desert** was covered with thin flakes that looked like frost. The people had never seen anything like this, and they started asking each other, 'What is it?' Moses answered, 'This is the **bread** that the Lord has given you to eat. And he orders you to **gather** about two litres for each person in your family – that should be more than enough.'

They did as they were told. Some **gathered** more and some gathered less, according to their needs, and none was left over. Moses told them not to keep any overnight. Some of them disobeyed, but the next **morning** what they kept was stinking and full of **worms**, and Moses was angry.

Each **morning** everyone **gathered** as much as they needed, and in the heat of the day the rest melted. However, on the sixth day of the week, everyone **gathered** enough to have four litres, instead of two. When the leaders reported this to Moses, he told them that the Lord had said, 'Tomorrow is the Sabbath, a sacred day of rest in honour of me. So **gather** all you want to bake or boil, and make sure you save enough for tomorrow.'

The people obeyed, and the next **morning** the food smelt fine and had no **worms**. 'You may eat the food,' Moses said. 'Today is the Sabbath in honour of the Lord, and there won't be any of this food on the ground today. You will find it there for the first six days of the week, but not on the Sabbath.' A few of the Israelites did go out to look for some, but there was none.

The Israelites called the **bread** manna. It was white like coriander seed and delicious as wafers made with honey. The Israelites ate manna for forty years, before they came to the border of Canaan that was a settled land.

8

Session 8

Moses went up *(tramping feet)* the mountain to meet with the LORD God, who told him to say to the people:

'You saw what I did in Egypt, and you know how I brought you here to me, just as a mighty eagle carries its young *(flapping wings)*. Now if you will faithfully obey me, you will be my very own people. The whole world is mine, but you will be my holy nation and serve me as priests.

'Moses, that is what you must tell the Israelites.'

After Moses went back, *(tramping feet)* he reported to the leaders what the LORD had said, and they promised, we will do everything the LORD has commanded. So Moses told the LORD about this.

The LORD said to Moses, 'I will come to you in a thick cloud *(whooshing sound)* and let the people hear me speak to you. Then they will always trust you.' Again Moses reported to the people what the LORD had told him.

Once more the LORD spoke to Moses: 'Go back and tell the people that today and tomorrow they must get themselves ready to meet me. They must wash their clothes *(clothes washing movements)* and be ready by the day after tomorrow, when I will come down to Mount Sinai, where all of them can see me.

'Warn the people that they are forbidden to touch any part of the mountain *(snatch back finger as though burnt)*. Anyone who does will be put to death, either with stones or arrows, and no one must touch the body of a person killed in this way. Even an animal that touches this mountain must be put to death. You may go up the mountain only after a signal is given on the trumpet' *(trumpet sound)*.

On the morning of the third day there was thunder *(rumble sound)* and lightning *(zig zag shape with hand)*. A thick cloud *(whooshing sound)* covered the mountain, a loud trumpet *(trumpet sound)* blast was heard, and everyone in camp trembled *(shiver)* with fear. Moses led them out of the camp to meet God, and they stood at the foot of the mountain.

Mount Sinai was covered with smoke *(whooshing sound)* because the LORD had come down in a flaming fire. Smoke poured out of the mountain just like a furnace, and the whole mountain shook *(shiver)*. The trumpet *(trumpet sound)* blew louder and louder. Moses spoke, and God answered him with thunder *(rumble sound)*.

The LORD came down to the top of Mount Sinai and told Moses to meet him there. Then he said, 'Moses, go and warn the people not to cross the boundary that you set at the foot of the mountain. *(Lift one leg and wobble, as if you are about to step, but don't OR hold up a finger as if warning someone.)* They must not cross it to come and look at me, because if they do, many of them will die. Only the priests may come near me, and they must obey strict rules before I let them. If they don't, they will be punished.'

Moses replied, 'The people cannot come up the mountain. You warned us to stay away because it is holy.'

Then the LORD told Moses, 'Go down and bring Aaron back here with you. But the priests and people must not try to push their way through, or I will rush at them like a flood!'

After Moses had gone back down *(tramping feet)*, he told the people what the LORD had said.

God said to the people of Israel:

'I am the LORD your God, the one who brought you out of Egypt where you were slaves.'

'Do not worship any god except me.' *(1)*

'Do not make idols that look like anything in the sky or on earth or in the ocean under the earth.' *(2)*

'Do not misuse my name.' *(3)*

'Remember that the Sabbath Day belongs to me.' *(4)*

'Respect your father and your mother, and you will live a long time in the land I am giving you.' *(5)*

'Do not murder.' *(6)*

'Be faithful in marriage.' *(7)*

'Do not steal.' *(8)*

'Do not tell lies about others.' *(9)*

'Do not want anything that belongs to someone else.' *(10)*

The people trembled with fear when they heard the thunder *(rumble sound)* and the trumpet *(trumpet sound)* and saw the lightning *(zig zag shape with hand)* and the smoke *(whooshing sound)* coming from the mountain. They stood a long way off and said to Moses, 'If you speak to us, we will listen. But don't let God speak to us, or we will die!'

'Don't be afraid!' Moses replied. 'God has come only to test you, so that by obeying him you won't sin.' But when Moses went near the thick cloud *(whooshing sound)* where God was, the people stayed a long way off.

Exodus 19,20 from the Contemporary English Version, adapted

9

**Session 9
Treasure box template**

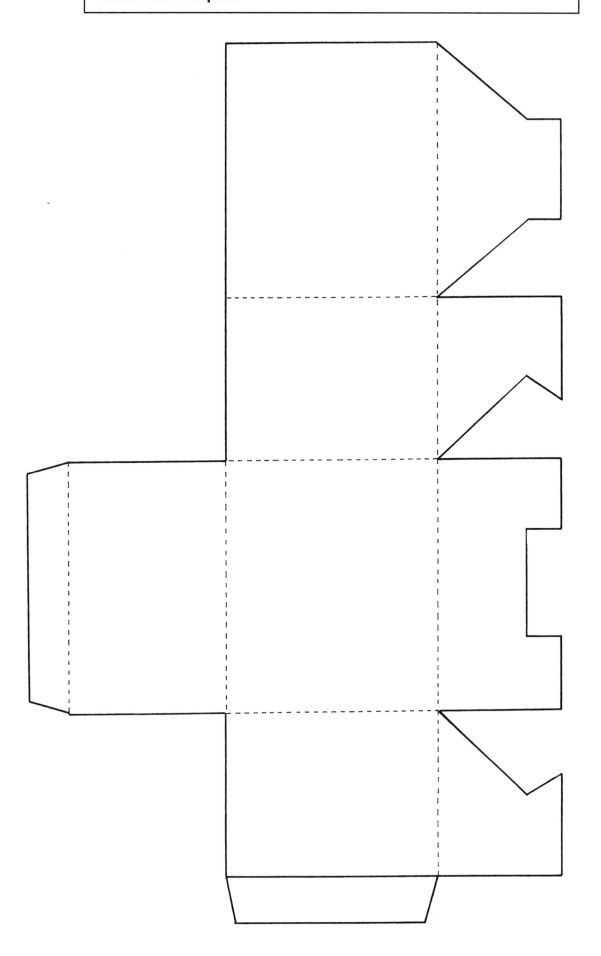

Session 9

These faces can be enlarged and attached to road cones (traffic cones or sports cones) to make figures to tell the story.

9

Session 9

Script to use to tell the story in the first person (adapted from Exodus 32:1–8,15–25,35 CEV)

You will remember how God gave us some laws while we were at Mount Sinai? Well, after we'd agreed to obey what God had said, Moses went back up the mountain with Joshua – his assistant – to collect the laws God had written on flat stones for us. He was on the mountain for a long time – so long that some of us thought he was never coming back!

One day a group of us went to see Aaron and asked him to make us a god to lead us and protect us. We knew that Moses said his God had brought us out of Egypt, but it's hard to believe in a god you can't actually see.

It didn't take Aaron long to realise what a good idea this was, so he asked us to bring him our gold and we all took off our earrings and gave them to him. Aaron melted the earrings down and then made them into the shape of a young bull. It was brilliant to be able to see god. Word quickly spread through the camp that this god had brought us out of Egypt. When Aaron saw how popular his golden calf was, he built an altar in front of it and told us all, 'Tomorrow we will celebrate in honour of the Lord.'

The next morning we got up early and killed some animals to be used for sacrifices and others to be eaten. Everyone was singing and shouting and dancing round the golden calf – really enjoying themselves. We ate and drank as much as we wanted. It was a great party!

Things were going well until Moses and Joshua arrived. Moses was carrying the two flat stones that God had written his laws on. When Moses saw us dancing around the idol he was so angry that he threw down the stones and broke them into pieces. Then he took the golden calf and melted it down and ground the gold into powder. While we all watched Moses scattered the powder in our water and made us drink it! And that wasn't all, because later God punished us with a terrible disease for talking Aaron into making the gold idol.

At first I didn't think it was fair that we were punished – we hadn't harmed anyone by what we'd done. Lots of nations have idols that they worship. But when I thought about it I realised – God had told us that we shouldn't have any gods apart from him. Even though Moses wasn't there God was still with us – we had seen him send plagues on the Egyptians, open the water of the Red Sea and every morning we ate manna that God provided. We should have trusted him more and believed in him and not done what we knew was wrong even though other nations do.

Session 9 Use to put the tail on the calf and for *Explore the Bible* 'Cone People'

Session 10
Template for disguise mask

10

**Session 10
Spies explore Canaan (Adapted from Numbers 13; 14:1-24, Joshua 1:1-9, CEV)**

Narrator: The Israelites moved their camp and arrived at the border of the Promised Land.

God: Choose a leader from each tribe and send them into Canaan to explore the land I am giving you.

Narrator: So Moses sent twelve tribal leaders from Israel's camp with orders to explore the land of Canaan.

Moses: After you go through the Southern Desert of Canaan, continue north into the hill country and find out what those regions are like. Be sure to remember how many people live there, how strong they are, and if they live in open towns or walled cities. See if the land is good for growing crops and find out what kind of trees grow there. It's time for grapes to ripen, so try to bring back some of the fruit that grows there.

Narrator: The twelve men left to explore Canaan from the desert in the south all the way to the towns in the north. When they got to Bunch Valley, they cut off a branch with such a huge bunch of grapes, that it took two men to carry it on a pole. That's why the place was called Bunch Valley. Along with the grapes, they also took back pomegranates and figs. After exploring the land of Canaan for forty days, the twelve men returned to Kadesh in the Paran Desert and told Moses, Aaron, and the people what they had seen. They showed them the fruit.

Spies: Look at this fruit! The land we explored is rich with milk and honey. But the people who live there are strong, and their cities are large and walled. We even saw the three Anakim clans.

Caleb and Joshua: Let's go and take the land. I know we can do it!

Other spies: Those people are much too strong for us. We won't be able to grow anything in that soil. And the people are like giants. They were so big that we felt as small as grasshoppers.

Narrator: After the Israelites heard the report from the twelve men who had explored Canaan, the people cried all night and complained to Moses and Aaron.

People: We wish we had died in Egypt or somewhere out here in the desert!

Narrator: Moses and Aaron bowed down and prayed in front of the crowd. Joshua and Caleb tore their clothes in sorrow. The crowd threatened to stone Moses and Aaron to death. But just then, the LORD appeared in a cloud at the sacred tent.

God: I swear that not one of these Israelites will enter the land I promised to give their ancestors. These people have seen my power in Egypt and in the desert, but they will never see Canaan. They have disobeyed and tested me too many times. But my servants Joshua and Caleb aren't like the others. So because they have faith in me, I will allow them to cross into Canaan, and their descendants will settle there.

Narrator: Ten of the men sent to explore the land had brought back bad news and had made the people complain against the LORD. So he sent a deadly disease that killed those men, but he let Joshua and Caleb live. Many years later, after Moses had died, the LORD spoke to Joshua son of Nun.

God: Now you must lead Israel across the River Jordan into the land I'm giving to all of you. I've commanded you to be strong and brave. Don't ever be afraid or discouraged! I am the LORD your God, and I will be there to help you wherever you go.

Session 10
Templates for Möbius Strip

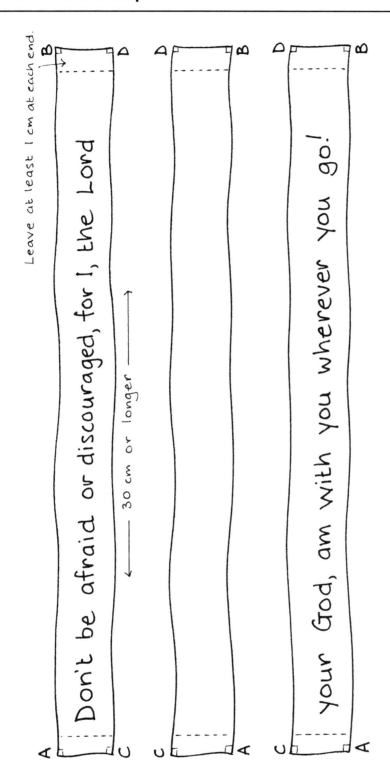

Leave at least 1 cm at each end.

Don't be afraid or discouraged, for I, the Lord

your God, am with you wherever you go!

← 30 cm or longer →

Write half the memory verse on one side of the paper, leaving at least 1 cm at each end. Words can be decorated.

Keeping the long edge at the bottom where it is, turn the paper towards you. The writing will be upside down on the underside. Write the second part of the verse on this side.

Make one twist of the paper and bring the ends together. Glue them in place.
Adapted from *Here's another one I made earlier* (Scripture Union) page 84.

eye level clubs...

- are for boys and girls aged 5 to 11.
- are for children who are not yet part of a church (as well as those who are).
- don't assume that children know much about Jesus or have had any experience of church.
- recognise that all children are open to God and the wonder of his world, and that all children can have valid spiritual experiences, regardless of church background.
- aim to give children one of the best hours in their week.
- provide opportunities for appropriate and respectful relationships between children and adults, working in small groups.
- plan to introduce children to the Bible in ways that allow for imagination, exploration and learning difficulties.
- are led by those who long to see children become lifelong followers of Jesus Christ.
- are led by those who will put themselves at a child's level, so that together they can catch sight of Jesus.